How to Afford Your Own Log Home

Save 25% Without Lifting a Log

by Carl Heldmann

The East Woods Press
Charlotte, North Carolina
New York • Boston

Library of Congress Cataloging in Publication Data
Heldmann, Carl
   How to Afford Your Own Log Home

   1. Log cabins—Finance. 2. Log cabins—Design and construction.
I. Title.
HD7289.A3H44 1984 643'.12 84-48037
ISBN 0-88742-012-5

Cover Illustration by Joel Tevebaugh
Typography by Raven Type
Printed in the United States of America

This East Woods Press book is available at special volume discounts for bulk purchases for sales promotions, premiums or fund raising. Special books or book excerpts can also be created to fit specific needs.

For details write the Sales Director, The East Woods Press, 429 East Boulevard, Charlotte, NC 28203.

How to Afford
Your Own Log Home

Contents

How to Afford
Your Own Log Home

The "Concord" from Greatwood Log Homes, Inc. is an open design featuring a loft and cathedral ceiling over the greatroom. This popular design permits the family to be together while three bedrooms provide private living areas, all within 1,872 square feet of living space. Greatwood offers a choice of traditional full log, or ultra insulated log building methods with an R-30 wall. Both systems include an R-40 roof system. (Courtesy Greatwood Log Homes, Inc.)

PREFACE

The incredible growth in the popularity of log homes is quite understandable. Log homes are beautiful, reasonably priced, energy efficient, easier to build, easy to maintain, very durable, a symbol of a person's spirit, and a spirit of, but a far cry from, log cabins of years gone by. The warmth of a log home is felt both from the outside and the inside. The richness of wood, our greatest renewable resource, is pleasing to the eye as well as to the pocketbook.

Study after study has proven that a log home is easier than most homes to heat in the winter and cool in the summer. Wood is a natural insulator! Studies show that it would take a concrete wall that is five feet thick to meet the insulating quality of only four inches of wood. Wood insulates six times better than brick, and an amazing 1,700 times better than aluminum. Why is wood such a good insulator? Wood is comprised of millions of tiny air cells. These air cells act like tiny vacuum bottles slowing the transfer of heat in either direction, keeping in heat in winter, and out in summer. Wood is also incredibly strong. Pound for pound, wood is stronger than steel. Log homes can, and do, last for centuries.

You can't go wrong with a well-designed and well-built log home. The manufacturers of today's log homes make it easier than ever to both obtain one and afford one. I hope you will find the log home of your dreams and I hope this book helps you afford it.

This interior is of the "Knoll," by Cedardale Homes, Inc. It features vaulted ceilings, stone fireplace with a stove insert and exposed beams. Carpeting, decorative interior wall coverings and furnishings add to the warmth and beauty of this contemporary log home. (Courtesy Cedardale Homes, Inc.)

INTRODUCTION

The subtitle of this book clearly states its purpose, to save 25% of the cost of your log home without lifting a log. It is the purpose of this book to show you that you can beat high interest rates, avoid a down payment, lower the amount of mortgage needed, or get a larger log home for your money while saving 25%, plus or minus, and all without doing any physical work. You can! You can do this even if you have a full-time job. If you elect to do some of the work, your savings could be even greater.

This book will show you how to acquire a log home by being your own general contractor. A general contractor is the person who hires the people who will build your log home. You will see that being your own general contractor is not difficult and is very rewarding, both monetarily and personally. No license is necessary for building your own log home, nor is any professional knowledge of the construction trade. A log home kit, or in some cases, an erected log shell, makes the job of being your own general contractor even easier. In most cases, you will have guidance from the log home manufacturer, another plus for you. You will also learn how to work with a professional general contractor if circumstances require it, and still save thousands.

In this book you will also learn some of the attributes of log homes. To learn more about any particular log home, you will need to contact some or all of the many log home manufacturers listed with addresses in the back of this book. A glance at the table of contents will show you that all you need to know is covered in this book. The National Association of Home Builders estimates that hundreds of thousands of people just like you will build their own homes this year alone. The North American Log Builders Association estimates that tens of thousands of people will build their own log homes this year. You can succeed! Good luck!

Note: Glossary terms are indicated by small capital letters.

PHASE I
THE PLANNING STAGE

Chapter 1
Being Your Own General Contractor

Most people, on hearing the term general contractor, conjure up a picture of a big burly guy hammering nails or laying brick. This may have been the case in years gone by, but it is rarely true today. Today's general contractor is more likely to be a manager of the time, people and money that go into the construction of a structure than the one who actually does the work. He employs the professional people, called subcontractors, to actually construct the house. The term builder is very misleading, for a general contractor or builder usually builds nothing himself. He manages the people who do. For this management function, he is paid quite well. You will be too, in the form of savings on the cost of your log home. Your savings can be used as your down payment, to lower the amount of mortgage you will need, thereby effectively beating high interest rates, or to get a larger log home for your money. Of course, you could elect to do some of the physical work yourself and save additional money, therefore being a subcontractor as well.

There are other reasons for being your own general contractor. You and you alone will guide the construction project towards your final dream. You will be more assured of getting exactly what you want and at a price you can afford. You will control quality and cost.

How Much Will You Save?

How much you will save by being your own general contractor will vary with each individual. There are many factors that govern your savings; the size of your log home, the price you pay for your land, the cost of labor in your area, and the cost of the other materials that will go into your log home. A savings of 25% is not impossible. Keep in mind that whatever you save, you will NOT have to earn and pay taxes on. This makes your savings even greater. NOTE: It's even a greater savings when you realize that you won't have to pay interest or repay principle on the amount you save.

A typical example of savings is shown below. As you will see, all financing figures are based on the appraised value, also called the market value, of an existing or proposed home. The following example is based on a 1,600-square-foot log home (heated area) in Charlotte, North Carolina. Costs are for 1984 and are approximate. They may be greater in some areas, but the percentages should stay the same. A chart comparing building costs in other parts of the United States can be found in the appendix.

EXAMPLE
1600 Sq. Ft. Htd. Area @$50/sq. ft.
    (retail, including real estate commissions) = $80,000
Actual total cost of construction = $48,000
Land cost = $12,000
Total cost of log home = $60,000
Your savings as general contractor = $20,000

This savings, which includes the real estate commission that you would pay, is equal to 25% of the appraised (market) value of this log home. As you will see in Chapter 6, you will be able to borrow the full $60,000 for construction financing, and the permanent loan, or mortgage. This means that you will have none of your own money invested in your dream log home . . . NO DOWN PAYMENT! Or, if you have money for a down payment, you could use that money to lower the amount of money you would need to borrow.

What Do You Need To Know?

The only major tools necessary for being your own general contractor are a telephone, a calculator and a checkbook. You need only to know how to organize your spare time and treat people in a fair manner, and you are in business. If that sounds simple, it is. You won't have to have technical knowledge of any of the fields of subcontracting, as your subcontractors are hired for their expertise in their fields. You don't have to know anything about plumbing to call a plumber to fix a leak or replace a defective plumbing fixture. The same holds true when you are building your own home. Your role as general contractor is that of manager of time, people and money. You already do this every day by managing the household budget, comparative shopping in the supermarket, balancing family time with work time, motivating people at work or at home, hiring repair people for various jobs, and so on.

You already have the knowledge to be your own general contractor. Keep this in mind throughout the process of building your home, especially when talking to lenders, and your confidence in yourself will show and be a help to you.

Here is a fine example of how log interiors adapt to contemporary lifestyles. American Lincoln also has a new line of contemporary homes featuring the look of beveled siding that blends beautifully into any residential setting while maintaining the natural beauty and benefits of solid wood construction. (Courtesy American Lincoln Homes)

This Cedardale home is the "Knoll." It features three bedrooms and two baths in 1,870 square feet. There is also an optional double car garage. Cedardale logs are tongue-and-groove and are made of Northern white cedar. Cedardale uses the well-tested post and beam method of construction. In addition to their many standard models, Cedardale offers a custom-design service and building seminars. (Courtesy Cedardale Log Homes, Inc.)

How Much of Your Time Is Required?

Consider the job of being a general contractor not as one large task, but as a series of little jobs, for that is what it is. Each little job in itself does not require much of your time. All of them can be carried out in your spare time. In the Planning, Financing, and Estimating Phases, you can proceed at your own pace, at your leisure if you wish. The Building Phase can also be handled so as not to interfere with your job or family life.

Planning can be done in the evenings or on weekends. The same holds true for estimating. Carrying out the first three phases of being your own general contractor is called doing your homework. By working with a log home manufacturer, a lot of your homework will be done for you. As we go through each phase, this will become evident. Other people can help you with your homework, as you will see. A quick example is using a real estate broker to check out all the things that need to be checked out before buying land. We will cover those in the chapter on Land. There are other helpers along the way. Some will help you free of charge, while others will charge a nominal fee. Any costs incurred are costs that all general contractors incur and are merely part of the cost of any home.

Do You Need a License?

You do NOT need a license to be your own general contractor for the purpose of building your own home. PERIOD! If you were to be a general contractor and construct a home for someone else, in most areas you would need a contractor's license and/or a business license.

Can You Get a Loan?

In Chapter 5 on Financing, you will see how to overcome the problems you might have in obtaining construction financing while acting as your own general contractor. This is mentioned now only because it is necessary to read this book thoroughly and more than once before you talk to prospective lenders.

Can You Do Your Own Labor?

If you are planning to do some of the physical work yourself, or have friends do it, be sure to check to see if any specific subcontractor license and/or permits are required. Most areas require plumbing, electrical, and mechanical (heating and air

This custom-designed log home addition was manufactured and built by Mountaineer Log Homes of Downingtown, Pennsylvania. Built as a custom addition to a turn-of-the-century log cabin, it features a loft and soaring cathedral ceiling. In its log homes, Mountaineer offers three varieties of wood: Northern white cedar, kiln-dried yellow pine and kiln-dried, pressure-treated (brown preservative) yellow pine. Mountaineer Log Homes also offers a custom log home designing service, planning assistance, one free day of building assistance and free freight delivery for the first 75 miles from the factory. (Courtesy of Mountaineer Log Homes, Inc.)

conditioning) work to be installed by licensed subcontractors.

Do You Need Permits?

In most areas, you will need certain permits, but they are easy to obtain and are not costly. The purpose of permits is to enable a local government to set up and maintain an inspection department. This inspection department is then responsible for the compliance with certain BUILDING CODES by all subcontractors. You will see that your local building inspection department is one of your helpers. If you don't have such a department in your locale, it will be explained in Chapter 8 how you can hire your own inspectors.

If You Can't Be Your Own General Contractor

If for some reason, even after carefully reading this book, you feel that you will not be able to be your own general contractor, then there is an alternative for you that will still save you thousands of dollars. It is called a MANAGER'S CONTRACT. An example is in the appendix. It is only an example. You would need to have a real estate attorney draw up a contract that would protect you and be binding in your state. A Manager's Contract allows you to hire a professional general contractor to perform any part of the process of being a general contractor. The more you want him to do and the more responsibility you give him, the more it will cost you. If you want him to merely do Phase IV, (the building stage) with the exception of buying from suppliers, he probably would charge you about half what he would charge if he were to do all four Phases. He would merely be "managing" your subcontractors for you. Of course, you could have him do more, but with an increase in his fee. You and a real estate attorney can make up your own Manager's Contract to suit your needs and in agreement with a professional general contractor.

There are two other forms of contracts in the appendix and they are there to show you two other ways to employ a professional general contractor. The "fixed fee" contract is usually the least expensive of these two, but certainly not as inexpensive as a Manager's Contract, as the professional general contractor's responsibilities are increased with the fixed fee contract.

CHAPTER 2
SELECTING A LOG HOME KIT

Selecting a log home is like selecting a new car. You will want to shop for what fills your needs. Cost, size, style, quality, ability to deliver on time, warranties, and references are some of the guidelines you should use in making your decision.

COST: Log home companies are very competitive in their pricing. In comparing costs, keep in mind the following: different kinds of wood, size of the logs (thickness), manner of construction, charges for plans, cost of freight to your job site, and what is included in the kit or package. This last item is, in my estimation, the most important. It is very difficult to compare "apples with apples" unless you know exactly what you are getting for your money. Will you be getting just the basic shell, or will you be getting everything necessary for DRYING IN the house? Does the basic kit or shell include the roof system, or just the rafters? Is the SUB FLOOR and its FRAMING MEMBERS included in the price? Can you buy the materials necessary for drying in the house locally for less? Will the log home company give you a list of these materials free of charge so that you can compare? In order to be fair to both you and the log home company, it is important that you ask these questions. You will find that company representatives are used to such questions and will be most helpful.

SIZE: We will discuss size fully in Chapter 4, but size is singularly the most important factor in determining price. You will need to consider it carefully. Most companies can offer any size log home.

STYLE: This is a very personal decision. There is a tremendous variety of styles available, both within each individual company and among the various companies. You should have no trouble finding a style to suit you.

QUALITY: Today's log homes are a far cry from those of yesterday. You will find that the quality offered by most log home manufacturers is excellent. You should, if at all possible, visit a model home to inspect for quality.

DELIVERY: Most companies give guaranteed delivery dates. Be sure that they do. When your subcontractor is ready for the kit, you want to be sure it will be there. The same holds true even if the company you buy from does the kit erection.

WARRANTIES: Again, most companies offer limited warranties. Check to see what the warranty covers.

REFERENCES: Obtain the names of people that have purchased homes from the companies you are interested in and call them. The Log Home Guide for Builders and Buyers (annual directory) is a good source for locating the log home company that is right for you. The address is: Muir Publishing Co., Ltd., 1 Pacific, Gardenvale, Quebec, Canada H9X 1B0, (514) 457-2045 or (705) 754-2201 or P.O. Box 1150, Plattsburgh, NY 12901. You can also find names of log home companies from advertisements, referrals and from the listing in the back of this book, reprinted with permission from Muir Publishing.

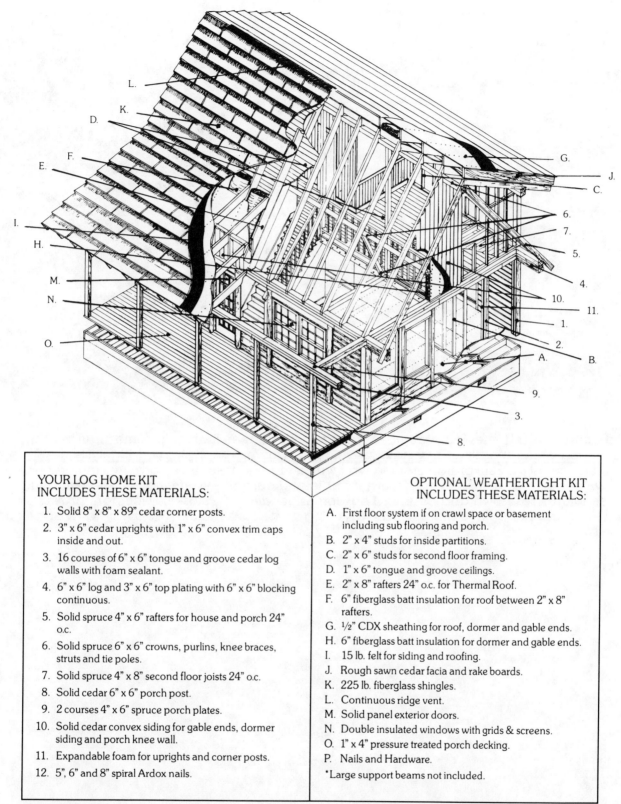

YOUR LOG HOME KIT INCLUDES THESE MATERIALS:

1. Solid 8" x 8" x 89" cedar corner posts.
2. 3" x 6" cedar uprights with 1" x 6" convex trim caps inside and out.
3. 16 courses of 6" x 6" tongue and groove cedar log walls with foam sealant.
4. 6" x 6" log and 3" x 6" top plating with 6" x 6" blocking continuous.
5. Solid spruce 4" x 6" rafters for house and porch 24" o.c.
6. Solid spruce 6" x 6" crowns, purlins, knee braces, struts and tie poles.
7. Solid spruce 4" x 8" second floor joists 24" o.c.
8. Solid cedar 6" x 6" porch post.
9. 2 courses 4" x 6" spruce porch plates.
10. Solid cedar convex siding for gable ends, dormer siding and porch knee wall.
11. Expandable foam for uprights and corner posts.
12. 5", 6" and 8" spiral Ardox nails.

OPTIONAL WEATHERTIGHT KIT INCLUDES THESE MATERIALS:

A. First floor system if on crawl space or basement including sub flooring and porch.
B. 2" x 4" studs for inside partitions.
C. 2" x 6" studs for second floor framing.
D. 1" x 6" tongue and groove ceilings.
E. 2" x 8" rafters 24" o.c. for Thermal Roof.
F. 6" fiberglass batt insulation for roof between 2" x 8" rafters.
G. ½" CDX sheathing for roof, dormer and gable ends.
H. 6" fiberglass batt insulation for dormer and gable ends.
I. 15 lb. felt for siding and roofing.
J. Rough sawn cedar facia and rake boards.
K. 225 lb. fiberglass shingles.
L. Continuous ridge vent.
M. Solid panel exterior doors.
N. Double insulated windows with grids & screens.
O. 1" x 4" pressure treated porch decking.
P. Nails and Hardware.
*Large support beams not included.

NOTICE: Some home styles differ in materials supplied with log kit. Please refer to price list for description of materials.

This is a cross section of a log home showing what is provided in a typical kit as well as what optional materials are available. This particular home utilizes post and beam construction. (Courtesy Cedardale Homes, Inc.)

Town and Country Log Homes is a group of experienced craftsmen that have come together from many facets of the log home industry. They have developed two very sophisticated log systems: Horizontal Triple Seal plus a Post and Sill pre-assembled wall with a high "R" insulative core. Two major ingredients, Northern white cedar and kiln-drying, insure a stable and durable system that is custom manufactured to precision tolerances. Town and Country Log Homes, located in Petosky, Michigan, provides model and plant tours and periodic seminars on the art of log home construction. (Courtesy Town and Country Log Homes)

CHAPTER 3
BUYING THE LAND

If you don't already own the property for your log home, one of your first jobs as general contractor will be to select and purchase (or contract to buy) the land. (One should note, this is one of the many things that you would have to do even if you were employing a professional general contractor.) If you already own your land, you may still find information from this chapter useful. Buying land is not a difficult procedure. Although buying land is a very personal decision, there are certain guidelines to help you. One of the most important is how much you should spend. The second most important factor should be the location of the property. Is it in an area where there is good resale value? Most people don't consider selling their dream log home before building it, but resale should always be weighed. You never know what the future will bring and if you someday find yourself needing to sell your home, you will want to sell it quickly and for the best price. The lenders you will be talking to will also be concerned with resale value. A real estate broker can advise you about the resale value of a particular location.

How Much Should You Spend on Land?

How much you spend is something only you can determine, but a good real estate broker can help with location. A good real estate broker can also help with some of the other things we will be discussing. Let's look at how much you should spend.

Unless price is of no concern, a good rule of thumb on how much to spend on your land is approximately 15% of the appraised or market value of the finished house. That may seem difficult to determine since you don't know what the market value is yet, but it is not necessarily complicated. If you have an idea of the size log home you want, you can determine approximately how much it will cost to construct the house by figuring a rough estimate (covered in the chapter on estimating), or by getting an estimate from the manufacturer or his dealer. Then work backward to determine market value. Let's use the example in Chapter 1, and the estimated cost of construction of $48,000. You

This log home, one of 17 standard designs and floor plans offered by Mountaineer Log Homes of Downingtown, PA, is called the "Powder Horn." The home features efficient design with excellent utilization of space. The Powder Horn is available in three different size floor plans. Mountaineer also manufacturers custom-designed log homes, garages, additions and commercial buildings. The company's standard log home kits are made of 7½"-thick, single tongue and groove logs, which are milled on all four sides. Two different log styles are available—Broad Ax (round exterior/flat interior) and Musket Barrel (round exterior/round interior). (Courtesy Mountaineer Log Homes, Inc.)

can see that land costs based on construction costs are equal to 25%, so you can simply multiply your rough estimate of $48,000 by 25%. This comes out to $12,000, which is 15% of the market value.

As you can see, the first three phases of being a general contractor intermingle. You will have to know how much money you can spend in total (covered in the chapter on financing) and how much the house itself will cost (covered in the chapter on estimating) while you are still in the planning stage. If you have to spend more than what is suggested, plan for it in your overall budget. The size of the log home is the largest determining factor, other than the land, in affecting total costs. If you have to pay more for the land, you may have to build a smaller home. This may be one of the many compromises that you have to make throughout your job as general contractor. There is nothing wrong with making compromises. Make them cheerfully during all phases of construction, and you will find your role as general contractor a pleasant one.

Zoning, Restrictions, and Other Deciding Factors

When buying land, be sure that what you see is what you will be getting. The use of a real estate broker is strongly suggested. You or your broker will want to check for the following: zoning, restrictions and utilities.

ZONING: This term is used to designate the use of a geographic area, as opposed to a single lot. It indicates where an area can be used for residential purposes, industrial use, commercial use, or farm use. The zoning may combine some of the uses or denote even other uses, depending upon where you live. Zoning is determined by local government. It is meant to protect. You are usually assured that the use designated today will be the same tomorrow. If an area is zoned residential, it means that a gas station cannot be built on that property. However, zoning can be changed and this is another reason to use a knowledgable broker. The broker should be able to tell by checking with planning commissions, zoning boards, etc., whether a certain area is likely to go through a zoning change in the future.

RESTRICTIONS: These are certain restraints placed on a particular lot or parcel of land by a previous owner, or by the present owner. Restrictions are usually found in subdivisions, but they can exist on any property. Some restrictions are very restrictive, so you or your broker need to check for them. They are most often RECORDED (filed) with the DEED. They could prevent you from parking a boat in your driveway, having a tool shed, hanging your wash outside, or they might restrict your house as to size or style, or a number of other things.

UTILITIES: You or your broker will want to see what utilities are available for your land. Utilities include water, sewer, electricity, telephone, and even cable television. Water and sewer can be from a city system or community system. Find out how much it costs to TAP-IN. If they are provided by a community system, be sure they are adequate and safe. You or your broker can check with the local health department or you can hire a professional engineering firm to check the system. Such a firm is likely to be listed in the Yellow Pages under Engineers—Sanitary, or Water, or some similar designation. If no water or sewer is available, or if one of the two isn't, you will need a well and/or septic system. Local health officials or a private firm will need to be consulted to determine if either a well or septic system is feasible for the land. You need to check with the local power companies to see how much it will cost you for them to provide electricity or gas to the land. The same applies to telephone and cable television. All this checking does not take a great deal of time, and if you let a broker do it, it will take none of yours. Just be sure that all meets with your approval before you finalize the purchase of the land. This can be done by having a provision in your contract to purchase the land that allows you sufficient time to check on everything before finalizing (closing) the sale. This provision, or clause, is called a contingency. If things don't check out to your liking, be sure that this contingency allows you to get back any deposit (binder). The contingency should also have a clause that allows you time to find suitable financing. Always use a contract to purchase the land. Your broker or a real estate attorney can provide one.

Other factors in deciding on land could be:

1. Feasibility for having a solar home. Will you be able to face the house in the right direction in order to take advantage of solar energy? Will large trees be blocking the sun and therefore have to be removed?

2. Do you want a sloping lot? A sloping lot will require more foundation, therefore, a higher foundation cost. A sloping lot, however, lends itself more easily to having a basement, and a basement that could have one or more walls open to daylight.

3. Do you want a lot with trees? Trees, especially large ones, enhance any home, and especially a log home, but clearing the lot for your home will cost more.

This "Lakewood" model, by Rocky River Log Homes, brings the outdoors indoors with 13 foot wide windows in the greatroom. This huge 36' by 14' room features a full cathedral ceiling and a large central fireplace. Three bedrooms, two baths, and a two car garage add the final touches. (Courtesy Rocky River Log Homes)

CHAPTER 4
HOUSE PLANS

Which comes first, the plans or the land, is not really that important except, as we saw in Chapter 3, you may need the plans to determine how much you should spend on the land. You can make almost any house fit on almost any lot. But when you are ready to look for plans, your job of looking has been made much easier for you by the log home companies. They offer an array of standard models that should please almost anyone's taste and budget. If not, most are willing and able to modify a standard model to your specifications, or do custom plans at a price far below what you would have to pay an architect or home designer for conventional house plans. Some will subtract any charges from the price of the kit when you buy from them. They all will work with you to assure you that you get the dream house you want.

How Big a House Do You Want?

Since the size of a home is the singularly most important factor affecting cost, it should be one of the first things you decide upon. How large a home to build is based on your needs and budget. You can usually determine space needs based on previous dwellings in which you have lived and by visiting model homes. It is, of course, a very subjective decision. What is large for one person may be small to someone else, and vice versa. If you are trying to keep overall size at a minimum, it is suggested that you keep the non-living areas as small as possible. These areas include bedrooms, baths, garages, and even kitchens. Instead of separate formal areas, you could instead have a large great room area. You could combine the kitchen with the dining area or den for a country kitchen look, thus eliminating space, and so on.

You will find your log home company representatives very helpful in assisting you with your decision. They can also, as mentioned in Chapter 3, give you a rough idea of what the finished house will cost, as they or their customers have built many. It can only be a rough idea because, as you will see, many other factors that go into finishing a house contribute to total cost and no two people will finish a house the same way or have the exact same labor or material costs. These and other factors and costs will be covered in Chapter 7. A general rule of thumb to determine the total cost of the finished house, not including land, is 2½ to 3½ times the price of the kit. This will vary depending upon what is included in the kit and local labor and other material costs. Ask the log home company what their general formula is. You are lucky! You wouldn't have such a rule of thumb in conventional stick building!

What The Plans Include

You will find that reading plans is not difficult. You are interested in size. Anything structural on the plans will be understood by your subcontractors. Anything that is too difficult for them to understand can be explained to them by the log home company.

Your final plans, called the blueprints, should include the following:

1. A foundation plan. Log homes can be built on any type of foundation, crawl space, basement, slab, pilings, or in some areas, an all-weather wood foundation. It should indicate the complete foundation from the FOOTINGS up to the SILL PLATE. It won't however, indicate the height of the foundation for a crawl space or basement, since that will vary with the slope of your land.

2. A floor plan for each level.

3. Exterior elevations for all four sides. Elevations are drawings showing what the outside of the building will look like.

4. A detail sheet. This shows a cross-section of walls, roofs, vaulted areas, location of cabinets, and a cross-section of any part of the house that may not be clear from the floor plan. This sheet can vary in detail and content. Check with your log home company.

5. A specification sheet. This will list the materials that go into the building of your log home, right down to the carpet. An example is in the Appendix.

Specifications (called specs) are a very important part of your plans. They list everything, including the logs, that will be going into your house. Included are the structural items as well as the decorative ones. The reason for having specifications is so that you, your lender, your suppliers and your subcontractors will know exactly what is going into your house. This is necessary for the purpose of controlling costs and quality. As you will see in Chapter 8 on subcontractors, as well as Chapter 9 on suppliers, getting accurate and competitive BIDS, CONTRACTS and QUOTES depends upon accurate specifications. There are other forms available and your log home company can help you complete any form you use. For some (or all) decorative items, you may not have made a selection, since specs come early in the planning process. In that case, you will need to budget a dollar amount for these items so that you can complete your cost estimate. For example, at the time the specs are completed, you most likely will not have selected carpet, wallpaper, stain colors, etc. But, by simply asking a supplier how much it is normal to spend on an item, or asking your log home company, or relying on previous experience, you can come up with a reasonable figure. You will be talking to suppliers early in the planning process, and in Chapter 9 you will see how to be assured that you are getting good advice and contractor's prices.

The "Countryside", by Brentwood Wood Log Homes, Inc., is a one story log home featuring a huge loft and exposed rafters. The loft has a dormer added to the back of the roof line to make it more spacious. The model above is an enlarged version of the "Countryside" with three bedrooms and two and one half baths which has 2100 square feet. This model is shown with 8" double tongue-and-groove super logs. All of these logs are machined for precision fit. These logs are available in kiln-dried yellow pine, Eastern white pine, and poplar. Three insulating materials are used between the logs. (Courtesy Brentwood Log Homes, Inc.)

PHASE II
THE FINANCING STAGE

CHAPTER 5
THE CONSTRUCTION LOAN

There are two phases in financing your log home. The first is the construction loan and the second, the permanent loan, or mortgage. The mortgage comes into play after your home is built and is discussed in the next chapter. The construction loan allows you to pay your subcontractors and suppliers during the construction of your home.

How you obtain a construction loan is discussed in a moment, but first, here is how one works. After you apply for and receive a construction loan, the money is disbursed (given) to you in stages, called DRAWS. These draws are in an amount equal to the percentage of completion of your home. For example, if at the end of the first month, your house is 25% complete, you will receive 25% of the amount of the construction loan. The percentage of completion is determined by the lender. Certain percentage points are given for certain items completed. A typical chart used by a lender to determine completion percentage is in the appendix. The draws you receive are usually sufficient to cover expenses, and you usually receive the draw before you even get bills for those expenses. You may have to pay some expenses prior to receiving a draw, but they are not usually more than a few thousand dollars. You will get the money for these expenses paid back to you when you receive the next draw. If you don't have a few thousand dollars to cover these interim expenses, you could borrow enough from a commercial bank on an interim basis (a short term note). Such an interim loan is not difficult to obtain, as the source of repayment will be your construction loan.

Paying For Your Kit

This is also a good way to pay for your log home kit, since it usually has to be paid for before you receive your first draw. However, some construction lenders will advance a draw for the purpose of paying for a kit. Be sure to check with your lender for their policy on this point.

The amount of money you can borrow for construction is usually the same as the permanent mortgage. When the house is completed, this mortgage will pay off the construction loan. In many cases, one lender can make both loans. The interest rate for a construction loan is usually a little higher than that of a mortgage, but it is a very short period of time. This interest is considered a cost of construction and is listed as such on the estimate of cost sheet in Chapter 7. You pay interest on monies received each month only. Not on the whole amount to be borrowed. Often construction loan interest can be paid out of the proceeds of the draws each month.

How to get a Loan

If you follow the following steps, you should be able to obtain your contruction loan acting as your own general contractor. You should have these steps completed before applying for your construction loan. Lenders will be more apt to make your loan if you do. You must show that you can do as good a job as general contractor as any professional can do. The lender's business is to lend money. Your job is to convince them they should lend it to you. If they see you are well prepared and eager to get started, you will be doing your job well.

1. Have your property either purchased or contracted to purchase with the contingency that you can obtain financing. If neither is possible at this point in time, then at least have your property selected.

2. Have your house plans and a Survey of your property.

3. Have an accurate cost estimate completed (See Chapter 7).

4. Have your major subcontractors lined up (see Chapter 8).

5. Have your suppliers lined up with accounts opened, if possible. (See Chapter 9).

6. Have proof of your income for the last two years, and a list of all debts and obligations.

7. If possible, have a letter of commitment for a mortgage. This will be discussed in the next chapter.

8. Have a positive attitude.

If one lender says no, try another. A lender's reluctance to make a construction loan to you acting as your own general contractor is usually based on fears that: 1. you will not be able to complete the project, leaving a partially completed home, and/or 2. the costs will run way over your estimate, making the home unaffordable to you. Since both of these things have occurred in the past, it is your job to convince them it won't happen in your case.

This is a modified "Woodstock" from Katahdin Forest Products. This fine home is 26' x 36' with a six foot deck across the front. An 18' x 36 living room with a cathedral ceiling highlights the inside. Extra high sidewalls provide enough room upstairs for two bedrooms and a bath. All together, there are 1404 square feet of living area including three bedrooms and two baths. All Katahdin homes are available in either cedar or pine. Custom-design service is available. (Courtesy Katahdin Forest Products)

Kits Make it Easier

Using a log kit or shell should help alleviate those fears, as you can control your costs more easily. Log homes are also easier to build and go up more quickly than most conventionally built houses. You can also show them pictures of finished homes, maybe even the one you are planning. That is something that's difficult to do with conventionally built houses. Be persistent, but pleasant. Remember, and you can remind the lender, that hundreds of thousands of people like yourself have done it, and will continue to do it. They got loans and you can, too.

The "Chatiemac," designed for year-round energy-efficient living by Lincoln Logs Ltd., Chestertown, N.Y., dramatizes the resurgence of an old answer to new housing needs. This 1,380 square foot home features three bedrooms, living room, dining room, kitchen and bath. It is one of 22 do-it-yourself log homes by Lincoln Logs Ltd. that can be built, without heavy equipment, in two weeks. The "Chatiemac" package includes double tongue-and-groove logs of Adirondack Eastern white pine, windows, doors, nails, spikes, caulking compound, between-log insulation strips, pre-fabricated roofing system, architectural blueprints. The kit comes with a 100-year warranty. (Courtesy Lincoln Logs Ltd.)

CHAPTER 6
THE PERMANENT LOAN

A mortgage is a loan that has the repayment stretched out over a very long period of time. Without mortgages, there would be very few houses in this country, as few people could afford them. Mortgages, however, have changed a lot in the last few years. The most notable change is that the interest rate charged for a mortgage has risen considerably, forcing many people out of the housing market. Another change is that there is now a wide variety of different mortgages available. The variety exists in order to help Qualify a potential borrower.

How Much Can You Borrow?

Qualifying simply means the lender thinks you can make the monthly payments on your home. Lenders use a variety of methods to make this decision. You can and should, as one of your first steps in planning your home, sit down and discuss mortgages with one or more lenders. They are the experts and their advice is *free*. They are some of the professional helpers mentioned earlier. You can discuss with them their requirements for qualification, various types of mortgages and their respective interest rates, and which would be best for you. This would merely be a preliminary meeting. At this time you are not applying for the mortgage. You are only trying to determine how much you can borrow, so you can determine how much house you can afford. Some real estate brokers call this pre-qualifying. Talk to more than one lender as there are differences from lender to lender. The more you learn from them, the more comfortable you will feel later when you do apply. If they also make construction loans, it is best at this time not to discuss construction financing, but rather to wait until you have followed the steps in Chapter 5.

No Money Down

After is it determined how much you can borrow, you can then determine how much house and land you can afford. For example (from Chapter 1): If you qualify for a $60,000 mortgage, you should be able to afford the $80,000 house in the example. If you borrow the full $60,000, the cost of both the land and the house are covered by the mortgage. You will be in your home with no down payment. You will want to have your construction loan in the same amount. Your construction lender may want you to pay for the land before they make the loan, but you will get that money back. Some construction lenders will make a land draw and pay off the land. Some construction lenders will allow the owner of the land to wait until you get your mortgage before they are paid. This is called a Lot Subordination. This arrangement would have to be worked out with an attorney and, of course, the land owner. You could also finance the land on a short term basis with a commercial bank. If you need to use the land as Collateral, this too would have to be handled as a lot subordination. Consulting with a real estate attorney will clarify all of this. Attorney's fees are also a cost of construction, so don't worry about spending dollars such as this for advice.

Obviously, if you want to put cash into your home, it would lower the amount of mortgage money (and construction money) needed. When you borrow less, your monthly payments are less, and you effectively beat the high interest rates. You also may put yourself into a better position for qualifying for a loan in the first place.

Letter of Commitment

If you are going to use one lender for construction financing and another for the permanent mortgage, you will need a Letter of Commitment from the permanent lender to present to the construction lender. This letter tells the construction lender that you have been approved for a mortgage. They then know that if they make a construction loan, it will be paid off. A letter of commitment can be obtained at any stage of your planning. You don't necessarily have to have selected land or plans yet. It is made to enable one to either go look for an existing house to buy, or, in your case, make arrangements to build. The letter will state that the finished house will have to pass final inspection by the lender. In the case of FHA/VA loans, not only will the house have to pass a final inspection, but also a series of inspections during construction. Again, you can discuss all this with a potential lender for further clarification.

The Gettysburg from Greatwood Log Homes, Inc. is a cozy three bedroom design with a friendly front porch. This affordable model has 1,700 square feet of living space and includes a spacious greatroom, large kitchen/dining area, and convenient lavatory/utility area on the first floor. The second floor contains a beautiful master bedroom with private bath and walk-in closet. The beauty and smooth, draw knife finish of a completely hand-peeled log is the reason Greatwood Log Homes specializes in the hand-peeled method. (Courtesy Greatwood Log Homes, Inc.)

PHASE III
THE ESTIMATING STAGE

This is the "Pathfinder" by Brentwood Log Homes, Inc. This Georgian style home exemplifies the American style country farm house found across rural America. This 2174 square feet of spacious living guarantees a life time of homespun living pleasure. Four bedrooms plus one full and one half bath on each level provides a family space to grow. The logs used in construction of this home measure 6" x 12" with a dove-tailed notch. The ceiling beams are 4" x 8" hand-hewn timbers. Logs are available up to forty feet in length and are West Coast hemlock or Eastern white pine. Poplar is also available. (Courtesy Brentwood Log Homes, Inc.)

CHAPTER 7
COST ESTIMATING

Estimating the cost of your log home will be one of your most important jobs as you act as your own general contractor. Your estimate will determine what you can buy and its accuracy will help you get your construction loan. Because you are building a log home, your job is made easier, as some of the hardest work is done for you by the log home company. In conventional construction, it is very difficult, if not impossible, to estimate all the materials that make up the exterior walls. How many bricks, or how much siding, or how many studs, or how much insulation, drywall, paint, trim, etc., go into a conventional wall is hard to guess. But in a log wall, it is all there. So are many of the other materials, such as the roof system, ceilings, and whatever else the company is providing. And you get a firm price on all of it.

Rough Estimating

For a quick, or rough, estimate, most log home companies have a rule of thumb they use to give you a rough idea of the cost of their finished homes. The rule usually is 2½ to 3½ times the kit price. This rough estimate is, as its name implies, approximate. It should only be used as a guide in the initial stages of planning. Another way to obtain a rough estimate is to use the average cost of construction per square foot for your area of the country. Your log home company's local representative should be able to give you that figure.

Accurate Estimating

The only way to get an accurate estimate is to get estimates on as many of the separate items that go into a house as you can. Listed below is an estimate sheet. In getting these estimates, you will be contacting suppliers and subcontractors, opening accounts and doing comparative shopping. When you have completed it, your role as general contractor will be almost over. You will have your plans, land, estimate, subcontractors and suppliers, all ready to begin construction. Following the list, each item is discussed.

The "Kenora" from Greatwood Log Homes, Inc. is an exciting design with 1,274 square feet of living space at an affordable price. An open floor plan with a loft and beamed cathedral ceiling makes this three bedroom plan one that is practical and beautiful. The wrap-around deck lends itself to easy entertaining and good times. Greatwood's "Country Retreat Series" contains dozens of designs that may be just right for you . . . be it a lake home, a starter home, a weekend retreat or a cabin in the woods. (Courtesy Greatwood Log Homes, Inc.)

SAMPLE ESTIMATE SHEET

	ESTIMATED COST	ACTUAL COST
ITEM		
1. Land		
2. Survey		
3. Plans and specifications		
4. Closing costs		
5. Insurance (fire)		
6. Construction loan interest		
7. Temporary utilities, permits		
8. Lot clearing and grading, lot staking and plot plan		
9. Excavation (for a basement)		
10. Footings		
11. Foundation, fireplaces, and chimneys		
12. Foundation waterproofing, soil treatment		
13. Subfloor (if not in kit)		
14. Log kit		
15. Log kit freight		
16. Additional framing material (if not in kit)		
17. Exterior trim (if not in kit)		
18. Windows and exterior doors (if not in kit)		
19. Kit erection labor (carpentry labor, including labor for subfloor and exterior trim)		
20. Roofing material (if not in kit)		
21. Roof labor		
22. Plumbing		
23. Heating and air conditioning		
24. Electrical		
25. Concrete slabs		
26. Insulation (if not in kit)		

27. Water and sewer (or well and septic)
28. Interior wall paneling or drywall—labor and
    materials
29. Interior trim and doors
30. Cabinets
31. Interior trim labor (carpentry)
32. Painting & staining (preservatives if necessary)
33. Appliances
34. Light fixtures
35. Floor covering
36. Drives, walks, and patios
37. Decks
38. Cleaning and trash removal
39. Wallpaper
40. Hardware and accessories
41. Landscaping
42. Miscellaneous, unforseen costs and cost overruns

With most of these items, you will be able to get accurate costs before you start building. With others you won't, but you can come reasonably close. As each item is completed during construction, you should enter its cost in the actual cost column next to the estimate. If the actual cost is more than the estimated cost, you can look for ways to lower costs in subsequent items. For example, you could use less expensive floorcovering or appliances. You can even eliminate some, like wallpaper, garage doors, etc. In this way, you have a reasonable amount of control over the total cost. Where to find each subcontractor is discussed in detail in Chapter 8. Below is a detailed discussion of the necessary items in your estimate.

1. Land. This is obviously an item that you will have a firm price on.

2. Survey. A survey will be required by your lender. Even if your lender did not require one, you should have a survey made of the property. A survey determines accurately the boundaries of the land you are buying. It should always be done by a registered surveyor. Cost will vary with the amount of land to survey, difficulty in locating corners and angles, and other variables, such as a surveyor's familiarity with the area. You can get a close estimate beforehand, however, over the telephone.

3. Plans and specifications. As with the land, you will have an accurate estimate of this item.

4. Closing Costs. These costs can be explained and estimated by a lender, even before you apply for your loan. They can be obtained over the telephone. These costs vary with the amount of the loan. They can consist of service charge, POINTS, attorney's fees for preparing the closing statements or documents and for certifying CLEAR TITLE, title insurance, prepaid fire insurance, preparing the TITLE, taxes, RECORDING FEES, and any other fees the lender may charge. The total for most closing costs is usually in the neighborhood of 3% of the loan amount. If you can obtain both the construction loan and the permanent loan from the same lender, you can save some money by avoiding duplication of some closing costs. Having two different lenders means having two sets of closing costs.

5. Insurance. You will be required by your lender to carry insurance on your home while it is under construction. This insurance is called a Builder's Risk Policy and it is necessary in the event of fire or damage. The extent of coverage and what exactly is covered varies with insurance companies. You should shop around by phone to get the most coverage for the least amount of money. Builder's Risk does not cover people. At the advice of your insurance agent, you may want to obtain a general liability policy in case someone other than a subcontractor is injured on the job site. Your subcontrctors will provide their own insurance coverage. It is very important that you be sure they provide you with a CERTIFICATE OF INSURANCE proving that they do have insurance. A copy of a typical certificate of insurance is in the Appendix. Your insurance agent can answer any questions you might have on insurance. You will have the exact cost for this item.

6. Construction Loan Interest. This amount can be estimated by a lender before you ever apply for the loan. The interest cost will vary with the size of the loan and the length of time it takes to complete your home. But a very close estimate can be obtained after you determine how much you are going to be borrowing.

7. Temporary Utilities, Permits, Lot Staking. You will need electrical service, water and possibly a portable toilet at your job site. Some local building codes require the toilet. A phone call to the building inspection department will let you know. Electrical service is provided by your electrician. It consists of a temporary meter, CIRCUIT BREAKERS, and receptacles, all mounted on a pole near the job site. This is called a SAW BOX and the electrical service is called SAW SERVICE. The electrician usually provides and installs the saw box free if he is to wire your house. The monthly bill for electricity is, of course, your responsibility. The charge per month is very small, and your local power company can give you an estimate. Water is provided by paying your local utility department for service and having your plumber install a spigot at the water meter. If you are going to

The "Elkhart" from Greatwood Log Homes, Inc. has a practical 1,500 square foot floor plan with a cathedral ceiling over the open and spacious greatroom area. Ample closet space and three bedrooms combine to make this design ideal. Greatwood's colorful planning guide contains one hundred models, ranging from 400 to over 4,000 square feet, including many passive solar designs. All designs can be modified, or their professional design staff will assist you with a complete custom plan. (Courtesy Greatwood Log Homes, Inc.)

have a well in lieu of water service, you will have to have it installed before construction begins, unless you can borrow water nearby. Fees for water service can usually be obtained over the phone from your local utility. Costs for a well are discussed in #27 below. A plumber usually will not charge for installing a spigot if he is to plumb your house. Permits that you will need and their costs can be obtained over the phone from your local building inspection department. Portable toilet companies are listed in the Yellow Pages, and a quick call will give you the monthly rental charge. Even if you are not required to have one, it is recommended that you do. It will help avoid embarrassing moments.

8. Lot Clearing and Grading; Lot Staking & Batter Boards. Your grading subcontractor can give you a contract price for this step after looking at your lot. He doesn't have to know exactly where the house is going to be positioned at this point. This step is discussed in Chapter 10, but be sure the contract price includes hauling away stumps, debris, rocks, etc. Later he will need to know exactly where the house is to be positioned on your lot and this is accomplished by placing stakes in the ground showing the outside corners of the house. This should be done by a registered surveyor/engineer, with your input, of course, as to where you want the house. The surveyor can give you a contract price. He may have to restake the house again after the clearing and grading, as the stakes may get knocked out of place. Be sure you discuss any charge for coming back. Prior to staking, he will draw your Plot Plan. Be sure to get a quote for that also. After clearing, your surveyor can install the Batter Boards.

9. Excavation. If you are going to have a basement, your grading subcontractor can give you a contract price after looking at your lot. Again, he doesn't have to know exactly where the house is going to be positioned at this time. After he begins grading, you may need your surveyor to check the work in progress as to the proper depth and side clearances for foundation work and waterproofing. (more on this in Chapter 10). Be sure to get a price from the surveyor for this.

10. Footings. A contract price for footings can be obtained in advance from your footing subcontractor. He may want to give you an estimate, however, since it is difficult for him to estimate exactly how much concrete and/or labor it will take. This is all right if he will give you a maximum amount that he will not exceed. Footings are explained in Chapter 10.

11. Foundation, Fireplaces, and Chimneys. Your brick and block mason subcontractor can give you only an estimate on these items. If he is good, he will come reasonably close. He will tell you how many bricks or blocks you will need as well as how much sand and mortar mix you will need to order, if he doesn't supply these items. He will tell you how much per brick and block the labor cost is, and your suppliers will tell you how much the materials cost. If fireplaces and/or chimneys are to be prefabricated, your supplier can give you a quote for the materials. Installation of them is usually done by your carpenters or a sheet metal company, or your heating and air conditioning subcontractor. All are capable of giving you a quote on the labor to install these items.

12. Foundation Waterproofing, Soil Treatment. You can get quotes from waterproofing firms listed in the Yellow Pages. Soil treatment firms are also in the Yellow Pages.

13. Subfloor. If your log home company is not supplying this, you can get a quote from a local lumber company. Often the log home company will give you a list of materials that go into the subfloor, but if not, the building supply company can make up such a list, called a TAKE-OFF, from your plans and specifications. If you are building on a SLAB foundation, see #25 below.

14. Log Kit. You obviously will have this price. Again, be sure of what is included in the kit, and for how long the quoted price is good. Be sure price is guaranteed long enough for you to complete all your planning, estimating, and financing arrangement.

15. Log Kit Freight. This amount can be calculated by the log home company. They will need to know where your building site is. If the site is such that large flat bed tractor trailers cannot get directly to it, be sure to allow some extra money for additional handling.

16. Additional Framing Materials. All that was said in #13 above applies here. Again, you have to know exactly what is and what is not included in your kit.

17. Exterior Trim. This consists of FACIAS, SOFFITS, moldings, GABLE trim, etc. Many log home companies include this in their kits as it affects the appearance of the finished product and by supplying these materials, they are more assured of enhancing the final appearance of their product. If not supplied, all that was said in #13 above applies here as well.

18. Windows and Exterior Doors. If not supplied with kit, a local building supply can do a take-off and give you prices. An exact amount can be determined. Be sure that screens and WINDOW GRIDS, SASH LOCKS, and storm windows and doors, if applicable, are included in prices. Prices can vary greatly by brand names, so shop carefully. Windows and doors are the greatest source of HEAT LOSS and HEAT GAIN, so insulated glass and/or storm glass is recommended and may be a requirement of your local power company. A phone call to the power company will inform you on this. They may

Virtually unlimited decorating possibilities await a Hearthstone Log Home owner. The massive hand-hewn timbers and 6' x 12' wall logs create a warm feeling alone, or when combined with your choice of wall coverings. Hearthstone offers a wide variety of floor plans and models which can be modified to suit every family's needs. Hearthstone also provides a skilled, professional erection crew to erect the log structure. (Courtesy Hearthstone Builders)

want to see your plans to calculate your requirements.

19. Carpentry Labor. You can get a quote from your carpentry subcontractor based on the square footage of your home. The quote should be for all labor involved in building the subfloor, erecting the kit, and drying the house in, exterior trim, and interior trim. Be sure to ask him if he charges extra for any items, and if so, these are to be explained to you, agreed upon and included in the quote. Extras might be: installing cabinets, prefab fireplaces, decks, porches, sliding doors, insulation, paneling, extra moldings, stairs, DORMERS, roofing, working at unusual heights, etc. You should also understand that any changes or additions to the plans and specs after you receive his quote will be an additional cost to you. Try not to make any, but if you do, obtain a revised quote.

20. Roofing Material. If roof shingles are not included in your kit, any building supply can do a take-off. They can also show you samples. Shingles vary greatly in price. A very close estimate can be obtained.

21. Roof Labor. If your carpenters do not install shingles, and a good many don't, a roofing subcontractor can give you a contract price. Price is per square of roof area. A square equals 10 feet by 10 feet of area, 100 square feet. Be sure that the contract includes any charge for FLASHING, installing RIDGE VENTS, and CAPPING.

22. Plumbing. Plumbing contractors should include all labor and materials to plumb the house including all fixtures, except appliances such as dishwasher, disposal, washing machine, but including the water heater. It is very important that your specs be very clear as to plumbing fixtures. A trip to a plumbing supply company or two will be necessary to select the fixtures that you want. The contract should also include any costs to connect water and sewer lines to their source.

23. Heating, Venting, and Air Conditioning—called HVAC. A firm quote is easily obtained for this item from your plans and specifications. Be sure that it includes any venting for bath fans, stove vents, furnace venting for gas or oil, dryer vent, and any other required venting.

24. Electrical. From your plans and specifications, an electrical subcontractor can give you a firm quote. It should include all switches, receptacles, wire, panel boxes, circuit breakers, the wiring of all built-in appliances, heat/AC, any exterior lights, and possibly security systems, intercom, and/or stereo wiring.

25. Concrete Slabs. This item pertains to basement or garage concrete floors. An exact quote can be obtained for the concrete work from a concrete subcontractor. It should include any reinforcing wire, styrofoam insulation, plastic film, and EXPANSION

Joints, as required by code. Any required fill dirt or sand, and stone for drainage under the slab, should also be included in the quote.

26. Insulation. Insulation will be required for subfloors, gable ends, roofs and ceilings, and dormer walls. An exact quote can be obtained from an insulation sub. If the insulation material is included with your kit, the labor to install can be contracted for with an insulation sub, or with your carpenters.

27. Water and Sewer, or Well and Septic. Your local utility company can give you tap-in fees. A septic system subcontractor, listed in the Yellow Pages, can give you an exact quote for your system. Local health officials, or private engineers, will determine its size and location on the property. Size and sometimes location affect price. A well driller should be able to give you an exact quote for a well. In some cases he may not be able to. Such circumstances could be rough terrain, rocky conditions, or unfamiliarity with local water tables. If he has to charge a price per foot drilled, it is recommended that he give you a maximum amount that he cannot exceed. Be sure that his contract includes the size well, pump, storage and recovery tank, and/or any necessary filters. Be sure also that he guarantees quality water at a sufficient yield.

28. Interior Wall Paneling or Drywall (labor and materials). From your plans and specifications, a building supply store can give you an estimate for materials for either paneling or drywall (sheetrock). Your carpenters can give you an exact quote on installing paneling and a drywall subcontractor can give you an estimate on installing and finishing drywall. Some drywall subs also supply the drywall. Be sure their estimate includes taping joints, and finishing with at least two coats of filler (called mud), sanding, and hauling away scraps, if possible.

29. Interior Trim and Doors. You will find a wide variety of styles and prices for these items. You will need to visit a building supply store to select them. They can do a take-off after you make your selection, and give you an estimate. Interior trim would include moldings, stairs, handrails, and shelving. Be sure to include interior trim selections on your specs.

30. Cabinets. This includes kitchen cabinets, bath vanities, and can include bookcases and such. An exact amount for all can be obtained from your plans from a building supply company or a cabinet maker, who can be found in the Yellow Pages, or by word-of-mouth. If the labor to install the cabinets is not included in the quote, get one from your carpenters.

31. Interior Trim Labor. Your carpenter can give you an exact quote based on your plans and specifications. It is usually based on a dollar amount per square foot.

Log home interiors appear to modern Americans seeking elegant but trouble-free living. Walls in this Lincoln Logs Ltd. "Chatiemac" are simply the machine-flattened interior sides of white pine logs naturally rounded on exterior sides. There's no interior covering or finishing. Yert the rustic look of natural wood compliments virtually every style. Moreover, the earthy colors and scent of logs create warm comfortable feelings, log home dwellers say. Even on a sunny spring day they can sense the magic of spending a winter's night curled up in front of a big stone fireplace surrounded by all the natural beauty. (Courtesy Lincoln Logs Ltd.)

Be sure it includes the installation of all the trim you selected, the cabinets, vanities and bookcases if necessary. As in #19, Carpentry Labor, you don't want to be charged for any extras at the end.

32. Painting, Staining and Preservative. You can obtain an exact quote for painting and staining as well as for log preservation, if necessary. Do not pay by the hour! Your quote should include labor and materials. As per the advice of your log home company, you may or may not have to have your logs treated with a preservative. If you do, they can recommend a company that should be able to give you an exact quote.

33. Appliances. Appliances to be included in the estimate are those that are considered built-ins. These would include dishwasher, range, ovens, and disposal. Prices vary considerably by manufacturer and model. You should shop more than one supplier, unless, of course, you know exactly what you want from previous experience. An exact amount for your selections is easily obtained.

34. Light Fixtures. This item usually includes flood lights, any decorative lighting, indirect lighting, door bells, intercoms, and security systems. Most lighting supply companies have sales people that can help you plan your needs and give you an exact quote. There is no charge for this service.

35. Floor Covering. All these estimates are arrived at by measuring the square footage needed from your plans. A floor covering supplier can give you an accurate quote for carpet or vinyl from your plans after you have made a selection. Price and quality will vary widely. If you don't wish to decide at this point, he can give you an idea how much you might want to use as an allowance figure in your estimate. For wood floors, you can obtain a close estimate by getting an estimate on the wood from a building supply company, a quote for installing from your carpenter, and a quote on sanding and finishing from a floor finisher. For slate, tile, stone, or brick floors, an exact quote can be obtained from a tile subcontractor found in the Yellow Pages.

36. Drives, Walks, and Patios. Depending on what these items are to be made of, concrete, asphalt, or crushed stone, an estimate can be made by a subcontractor from a copy of your PLOT PLAN, which is a copy of your survey showing where the house will be located on the lot. Your input will be required as to widths, size, length and materials used. One subcontractor may be able to give you a quote using any material. Quotes should, of course, include all labor and materials.

37. Decks. Decks should be shown on your plans, and if they are, a building supply can do a take-off as to materials. As mentioned in #19 above, decks are usually an extra with your carpenter. He can, however, give you an exact quote.

38. Cleaning and Trash Removal. If you have never had a house built before, you might wonder why you have to clean a new house. The amount of trash generated will amaze you. However, any of the professional cleaning service companies in the Yellow Pages can give you an exact quote for cleaning, even from your plans. Their cleaning should include windows, both sides, bathrooms, cabinets, and everything inside the house. These companies, in most cases, can include trash removal in their quote. If not, your landscape subcontractor or your grading subcontractor from #8 above can give you an estimate based on previous experience.

39. Wallpaper. Any wallpaper store can give you an estimate of what an average allowance might be from your specs, since you probably won't be selecting your wallpaper just yet. When the time comes, they can give you assistance in selection and help in determining the amount of paper necessary.

40. Hardware and Accessories. This will include door knobs and locks, door stops, towel bars, mirrors, etc. A building supply company can give you an estimate from your plans of what an average allowance would be. Prices vary considerably and you can spend anywhere from a few hundred dollars to thousands on this item.

41. Landscaping. After looking at your land, where the house will sit, and discussing what you want or need, a good landscape subcontractor can give you an exact quote.

42. Miscellaneous. It is impossible to plan for every cost in construction, so allow for it. Take the total of the first 41 items and multiply by 5%. This should allow not only for unforseen costs, but most cost overruns as well. In addition to this, add for any items not included above, such as garage doors, stone work, swimming pools, CHINKING, etc., that may apply to your home.

The "Katahdin" by Katahdin Forest Products is a ranch style log home with 1768 square feet of living space. Utilizing the lay of the land enabled a double car garage to be built under the right wing off this house. The main wing features a cathedral ceiling and large fireplace that separates the living area from the kitchen and dining area. Katahdin offers custom-design service and their homes are available in cedar or pine. You can purchase the logs only or a complete weather tight kit. (Courtesy Katahdin Forest Products)

PHASE IV
THE BUILDING PHASE

CHAPTER 8
SUBCONTRACTORS

In this chapter we will discuss how to find good subcontractors, how to contract with them, how to schedule them, how to work with them, how and when to pay them, and how to inspect their work.

What is a Good Subcontractor?

A good subcontractor is one who does quality work at a reasonable price and is reliable. Determining quality is somewhat subjective. What one person considers good work, another may not. There is no perfection in construction, but as long as you and your team of inspectors, whom we will discuss below, are satisfied, that is all that should matter. If a sub does quality work for one general contractor, he usually does so for another, as he depends on good references for his livelihood. This points out the importance of getting and checking references. It is recommended that you get at least three references for each subcontractor you are planning to hire. If any sub refuses to give references, find someone else. In checking references for quality, you can also check on a subcontractor's price and his reliability. Reliability can be as important as quality. If a sub does not show up when scheduled, he can hold up your entire job. This costs you money in construction interest.

Finding Good Subcontractors

There are several ways to find good subcontractors. Here is a list of most, if not all, of the subcontractors you will need and how to find them. NOTE: In various parts of the country, subcontractors may be called by different names.

1. Real Estate Broker. You can find a broker from the brokers' ads in the newspaper, word-of-mouth referral, Yellow Pages. You may need one to purchase your land.

2. Attorney. Find on the referral of friends, real estate firms, or lending institutions, or from the Yellow Pages. A real estate specialist will work faster for you.

3. Lending Officers. These people will be at the banks that will be loaning you money, both for construction financing and permanent financing. No references are necessary here.

4. Insurance. You can use the insurance agent you now use for car insurance, renters' or homeowners' insurance, etc.

5. Surveyor. You can find through the Yellow Pages, on referral from real estate firms, attorneys, or lenders. Be sure the one you choose is licensed (registered) and insured.

6. Log Home Company. The Log Home Guide for Builders and Buyers Annual Directory is a good source for locating the log home company that is right for you. The address is: Muir Publishing Co., Ltd., 1 Pacific, Gardenvale, Quebec, Canada H9X 1B0, (514) 457-2045 or (705) 754-2201. You can also find names of log home companies from advertisements, referrals and from the listing in the back of this book, which was reprinted with permission from Muir Publishing.

7. Carpenter. This is one of, if not the, most important of your subcontractors. It is recommended that you line him up early in the planning process. He is also a good source for finding other subcontractors that you will need, as he works with most of them every day and knows both the quality of their work and their reliability. It is wise to get a carpenter that has erected a log home before, and preferably, one of the kind you are buying. The log home company's representatives often have names of carpenters familiar with their product. If the company is to erect the shell, you will still need a good carpenter for trim, decks, etc. Other ways to find this subcontractor are: from a building supply company, real estate firm, referral from friends, or by stopping by a job under construction. You could also call a general contractor whose homes you have seen and whose workmanship you have admired. It's done all the time. Many general contractors don't build enough homes in a year to keep their carpenters busy full time. They shouldn't mind giving you the name of their carpenter as you are building only one house and will not seriously affect his scheduling of future jobs.

8. Grading and Excavation Subcontractor. Found through referrals from friends, your carpenter, real estate brokers, the Yellow Pages, sand and gravel suppliers listed in the Yellow Pages, from a job under construction, or from a professional general contractor.

9. Footing Subcontractor. This sub is often the same as #8, but, if not, you can use the same sources as outlined in #8. In different parts of the country, different types of footings are used and different names are applied to the process of this beginning

This photo of a variation on a standard "Garrett" model produced by Mountaineer Log & Siding company illustrates the versatility that their custom-design services offer the log home purchaser—virtually any style or floor plan can be adapted to log building. This mid-Atlantic based manufacturer delivers complete exterior packages including logs, windows, doors, floor, roof, and more on a 3–4 week delivery schedule. (Courtesy Mountaineer Log & Siding Company)

of your structure; for example, pilings are used in some parts of the country in lieu of footings.

10. Brick and Block Masonry Contractor. This is the subcontractor that will build your foundation. Carpenters often know good brick masons. Also, referrals from friends, brick suppliers, professional general contractors, Yellow Pages, or by stopping by a job in progress, are ways of finding this sub.

11. Waterproofing Subcontractor. For waterproofing your foundation, it is recommended that a professional company listed in the Yellow Pages under Waterproofing or another such heading is used to do your work. Most anyone can do the job, but they may not guarantee their work. Water problems can be quite a bother, so it is best to have a pro take care of them early.

12. Roofing Subcontractor. Use the same sources as #7 and the Yellow Pages.

13. Plumbing Subcontractor. You can get referrals from plumbing suppliers, friends, your carpenter, a job under construction, Yellow Pages, or other general contractors.

14. Heating and Air Conditioning and Vent (HVAC). Same as #13 and the Yellow Pages.

15. Electrical Subcontractor. Same as #13 and from an electrical supply company.

16. Concrete (Finisher) Subcontractor. Same as #7.

17. Insulation Subcontractor. From the Yellow Pages.

18. Drywall Subcontractor. Same as #7.

19. Painter. Same as #7.

20. Flooring Subcontractor(s). Same as #7 and in the Yellow Pages. This sub is usually a supplier.

21. Cleaning Service. Same as #7 and in the Yellow Pages.

22. Wallpaper Hanger. A wallpaper store is usually a good source for this subcontractor, as are the sources listed in #7.

23. Landscaper. Same as #7 and in the Yellow Pages.

Subcontractor Bids and Contracts

Subcontractors contract with you to perform a certain task at an agreed-upon price (quote or bid). Because of this arrangement, they are not considered your employees by the government, so you needn't worry about withholding taxes. You will need to file a Form 1099 with the IRS on all subcontractors that aren't corporations.

Town and Country Log Homes refines a variety of special wood interiors. Post and Sill walls are milled to a furniture finish with interior options of cedar, cherry, ash, pine or Balm of Gilliad. Precisely-cut roof systems are available with log rafters, king post trusses with log purlins, or scissor trusses with log purlins (pictured above). All systems are on display at the Town and Country plant in Petosky, Michigan. (Courtesy Town and Country Log Homes)

This form merely shows how much money you paid them.

A sample subcontractor's contract is in the Appendix. It is merely an example. You should have your attorney draw one up for your use. You will notice that the contract provides spaces for the quote, work to be performed, insurance information, and the terms of payment. It is recommended that you get three or four quotes or bids, based on your contract form, from each type of subcontractor. To be sure that you are comparing "apples with apples" when getting quotes, be sure your form is followed explicitly. Also, never pay any subcontractor by the hour rather than by the job. It is too easy to go over your budgeted allowances with subcontractors who work and are paid by the hour. Make sure that your specs clearly state the materials each sub is to provide if those materials are to be in his contract. By getting three or four bids, you can also get a better feel for costs in your area.

Scheduling Subcontractors

Scheduling your subs is not difficult and should require little of your time. In most cases, they will be scheduled in accordance with the sequence of building steps in Chapter 10. After you have accepted a subcontractor's bid, you can let him know when you will need him, based on where he fits in the sequence, and when you plan to start. There is an estimate of time for each step, so you should be able to give him a rough idea. Most scheduling is done by phone in the evening or on weekends, so your time involved is minimal. After construction begins, you can schedule better. Some of your subs might keep an eye on job progress for you, in order to schedule themselves. You can ask if they would be willing to do this. If one subcontractor can't fit into your schedule after you start, then you will have to decide whether to wait for him or find another to do the job for you. If it is going to be a long wait, more than a few weeks, you might be better off finding another. Your decision will also depend on how much of your house has been completed. In the beginning, the construction interest that you are paying is minimal, but later in the process of building, it is higher. You can't afford to wait too long when the house is nearly completed and your interest payments are higher.

Working With Your Subcontractors

If you have done your homework carefully and have checked references carefully, the best way to work with your subcontractors is to leave them alone. Let them perform their jobs. They are the pros. If they have a question or need something, have them call you. You might want to install a job phone. It is inexpensive and will save you and your subs time. It can be locked up at night or taken home.

Paying Your Subcontractors

In the sample contract, you will notice the space provided for terms of payment. Terms of payment vary for different subcontractors and vary also with different locales. But one good rule to follow is, never pay for anything in advance! Pay only for work completed. However, some subs will need to be paid on a *weekly* basis, and some when a certain part of their total job is complete. If a sub needs a weekly payment, called a draw, then *you* will have to determine what percentage of the contracted job has been completed. It really is not difficult, but let common sense prevail.

The subcontractors that might need a draw usually are brick masons, carpenters, and painters. If, for example, your carpenter is halfway completed trimming out your house (he has installed one-half of the materials you ordered for trim), you can give him up to one-half of his contract price for trimming. Actually, a little less would be better, and ten percent less than one-half is the norm. If your brick mason has laid a certain number of bricks or blocks, that is what you pay him for, less ten percent. The amount of draw to release to your painters is more of a "guesstimate," but be careful not to overpay.

Subcontractors that are paid for a part of their job are electrical, plumbing and HVAC subcontractors. When their Rough-Ins are complete and have been inspected, you will pay them a pre-agreed-upon percentage of their total quote. Be sure that this amount is in their contract. All other subcontractors are paid after they have completed their work, and that work has been inspected. Some subs (other than the ones requiring draws) can wait until you get your construction draw (thirty days or less) before getting paid, and this is to your advantage. Ask when discussing terms of payment in the contract.

Inspecting a Subcontractor's Work

In most areas there are building inspectors that inspect the critical stages of construction for quality and compliance with codes. If not, you can hire private professionals to inspect the work on your home. Other less critical stages of construction, such as painting, can be inspected by you, using your good common sense. Payments due to subcontractors should be made only after inspection of the work they have done. Inspections that are usually performed by your local building inspection department or professional inspector might be:

1. Temporary electrical service (saw service).
2. Footings, done before the concrete is poured.

The rustic beauty of a log home is enhanced by a modern custom-designed kitchen. Kitchen cabinet packages are just one of the options available through Mountaineer Log & Siding Company to totally customize your log home. You can also choose from Kiln-dried, CCA-salt-treated, or air-dried logs. (Courtesy Mountaineer Log & Siding Company)

3. Foundation.

4. Well and septic systems.

5. Concrete slabs, done before the concrete is poured.

6. Electrical, plumbing, HVAC Rough-Ins.

7. Structure, called framing inspection in conventional building. This is performed after the subcontractors in #6 are finished, to check for structural soundness.

8. Insulation.

9. Final inspections for: electrical, plumbing, HVAC, and the structure again to be sure that all codes are complied with and that everything works and is safe. In areas where there are building inspection departments, you probably will have to have completed #9 before you can get permanent electrical or gas service. Your lender may require the same inspections before permanent financing is given.

There may be other inspections required in your area. They are for your protection. If at any time you are in doubt as to whether or not a job is done properly, call your building inspector or hire a professional inspector and find out. Professional inspectors may be called "Home Inspection" firms or engineering firms. In some areas, you will find home inspection firms listed in the Yellow Pages. They can usually perform any necessary inspections. In other areas, firms may be listed in the Yellow Pages under specific headings for the specific inspections they perform. Most firms are listed under the heading "engineers' and followed by their specialty, i.e. foundations, HVAC, consulting, etc. You can also hire an architect for any inspections or a professional general contractor.

Don't worry about spending money for inspections, even if it is in the hundreds of dollars. You are saving thousands by being your own general contractor and these inspections will give you the assurance that your home will meet the codes and standards that both you and the building inspection department set for it.

CHAPTER 9
SUPPLIERS

Other than your log home company, you probably will be buying from some or all of the following suppliers:

1. Sand and gravel company. For sand for your brick masons, dirt for BACKFILLING and landscaping, gravel for drives, etc. Some subs supply these items, so you may have no need for this supplier.

2. Block supplier. For foundation block.

3. Brick supplier. For face (decorative brick for foundations, chimneys, etc.)

4. Concrete supplier. Many concrete subcontractors furnish concrete in their contract price.

5. Building supply company. For any framing materials not included in your kit, and/or doors and windows, etc., if not included. Also for interior trim, and many of the items carried by the suppliers listed below.

6. Floor covering supplier. For flooring needs, and usually for counter tops as well.

7. Light fixture supplier or electrical supply company.

8. Paint store. To select colors only. Paint is usually supplied by the painter in his contract price. Paint stores also carry wallpaper.

9. Appliance store.

10. Tile company. For tile, slate, marble, and decorative stone.

11. Specialty stores for items such as solar energy systems, fences, etc.

Opening Accounts And Getting Discounts

To be able to buy supplies at a builder's discount, you will need to open a builder's account with each supplier. This is not difficult. All you have to do is explain to the management that you are "building" a house, and that you would like to receive a builder's discount. Simple as that! They now know you are not just a weekend do-it-yourselfer, buying in small quantities. They also know that many of their professional accounts started out just like this. Builders' discounts vary, and in some cases are very small. But it all adds up. So does the sales tax, and it is completely tax deductible, another savings for you. To open an account with a supplier, you most likely will need at least three credit references, such as Sears, and a bank reference. They may also want you to inform them of your construction lender when you get one. Their terms of payment are quite different from Sears, as you will see.

Paying Your Suppliers

Most suppliers who deal with professional general contractors on a daily basis have their terms of payment set up to aid the general contractor. Payment for supplies purchased in one month is not due until the following month. This allows the general contractor, you, to have time to get a construction draw. For example, if you purchased brick on June 1, it may not have to be paid for until July 30. Usually a 2% discount is given if you pay by the 10th of the following month, July 10th in this case. Always ask if a discount is given, because often it is not stated on the invoice or monthly statement.

Bookkeeping

Since you are only building one house, a check book should provide sufficient bookkeeping records. You can transfer amounts from your check register onto the actual cost column of the estimate sheet. You should, of course, open a separate checking account to be used solely for payment of construction bills. If you want to use a more refined means of record keeping, fine. A home computer could be utilized, or simple accounting forms from an office supply. Do be sure you keep a record of any sales taxes paid, as you can claim these taxes on your personal income tax.

Hearthstone's picturesque "Continental" model captures the rustic charm found in log home living. Featuring a cathedral ceiling in the kitchen wing, this authentic, hand-hewn home offers three roomy bedrooms, two full baths, and a first floor utility room for a total of over 1,500 square feet of living space. Every Hearthstone home is hand-hewn by Appalachian craftsmen, using a foot adze. This not only creates an authentic home, but squaring the timbers leaves more of the heartwood, which is naturally resistant to decay, insect attack, and log shrinkage and twisting. (Courtesy Hearthstone Builders)

CHAPTER 10
BUILDING YOUR HOME

When you reach this point, your work as a general contractor is almost complete. Now your team of professionals can go to work and build your dream log home. In this chapter, the sequence in which your home will be built is discussed and the average time for each step is indicated. Actual time to complete any step will vary due to factors such as weather, different techniques of construction, and various other reasons.

Steps of Construction

Here is a list of the steps of construction. Each step is discussed following the list.

1. Ordering the kit or shell and getting permits: 1–3 hours.
2. Staking the lot and house: 1 day.
3. Clearing the excavation: 1 day to 1 week.
4. Ordering utilities, temporary electrical service, portable toilet, getting insurance. 1–3 hours.
5. Footings. 1–2 days.
6. Foundation, waterproofing, and soil treatment. Call for a foundation survey when complete. 1 day to 2 weeks.
7. Plumbing rough-in if slab foundation. 2–4 days.
8. Slabs. 1–3 days.
9. Kit erection and drying in, exterior trim. 1–3 weeks.
10. Chimney and fireplace(s). 1 week.
11. Roofing. 1–3 days.
12. Plumbing, HVAC, and electrical rough-ins. 2 weeks.
13. Insulation. 2 days.
14. Hardwood flooring and carpet underlayment. 2–5 days.
15. Drywall or paneling. 2 weeks.
16. Interior trim. 1–3 weeks.
17. Painting and staining. 2–3 weeks.

18. Tile, counter tops, etc. 1–2 weeks.
19. Trim out plumbing. 2–4 days.
20. Trim out HVAC. 1–2 days.
21. Trim out electrical. 2–4 days.
22. Floor finish and/or carpet. 2–5 days.
23. Clean up. 2–3 days.
24. Drives and walks. 2–4 days.
25. Landscaping. 1–3 days.
26. Final inspections. 1–2 days.
27. Loan closing. 1 hour.
28. Enjoy. A lifetime!

The Steps Explained

1. Ordering the kit or shell. Your log home company should inform you how far in advance you need to order your kit or shell. When your foundation is completed, you will want to have your kit there or on its way. By reading this chapter and discussing schedules with your subs, you can approximate reasonably well when this time will be. If something delays that time, shipping can be delayed. Most companies will work closely with you on delivery dates.

At this time you should obtain any necessary permits. A call to your building inspection department and/or health department will inform you of the necessary permits and the procedure to follow in obtaining them. It can most often be done on a lunch hour or two.

You can also arrange for your Builder's Risk insurance at this time. It needs to be in force prior to starting construction.

2. Staking the lot and house and installing batter boards. Your surveyor should check to see that all boundary stakes are accurate. They could have been moved since you purchased your land. Then you and he can determine precisely where the house will "sit" on the lot and you will place stakes showing all the corners of the house. This can be done on your lunch hour, after work, or even on the weekend. Your surveyor will make sure that your house is not in violation of any setback restrictions. The corner stakes will let your clearing and excavation subcontractor know where to clear and/or excavate. Usually the surveyor will also place offset stakes indicating the corners far enough away so that they won't be disturbed, and the actual corners can be relocated if need be. Your surveyor can also guide your decision how to position the house so

The "Vinyard," a four bedroom two and one-half bath stately home by Rocky River Log Homes, features large rooms, a country kitchen, a large master bath with room for a sauna, a great room and a den, and a garage with a recreation room above. Total living area is 3,520 square feet. (Courtesy Rocky River Log Homes)

that water drains away from the house. He can also help determine best positioning for solar energy considerations. He can install your BATTER BOARDS now or at any time prior to #6. If they might become damaged during steps 3–5, it might be best to wait.

3. Clearing and excavation. If your lot is heavily wooded, be sure you clear enough area around the house so that there is enough space for tractors and forklifts to operate. In some areas, local codes require a certain amount of cleared space. A quick phone call can tell you if this is the case. If you are having a basement dug, you may want your surveyor to supervise to be sure of proper depth. Be sure your contract price with your clearing and excavation subcontractor includes hauling away all trash and debris.

4. Utilities. Your subs will need water and electricity, so now is the time to have your saw service installed, water connection made, or well drilled. In some cases, this is an excellent time to install a septic system. Check with your subcontractor.

NOTE: BE SURE YOU HAVE ORDERED
YOUR BUILDER'S RISK INSURANCE!

5. Footings. Types of footings vary as to locale, but they are usually made of concrete poured in trenches or forms. They can also be in the form of pilings, or in a combination of footing and concrete slab together, called a monolithic slab. Your plans will show clearly what type of footing you will have. Since footings form the basis of your house, you will want to have this step inspected. If your county doesn't have a footing inspector, hire a professional inspector. You might also want to have your surveyor check to see that the footings are the exact dimensions of the house and that they are in the right place, although you could do this. Footing inspectors will check for proper depth and to be sure that the footings are on solid LOAD BEARING ground. They also check to be sure that they are below the point where the ground freezes, called the frost line. Footings are inspected before the concrete is poured.

6. Foundation. As mentioned earlier, your log home can be built on any type of foundation. The foundation can be made of brick, block, poured concrete, concrete slab, pilings, and all-weather wood foundations. You can have your carpenter or surveyor check the foundation for levelness and squareness if you like. Be sure that the crawl spaces are high enough. Most codes require a minimum of 18 inches. Be sure that the basement walls are high enough so that you will have sufficient head room. Be sure that any foundation is high enough so that water can be diverted around it and that no portion of your wood walls are closer than 8 inches to the finished grade.

After the foundation is finished and, in the case of a concrete slab, before the concrete is poured, you or your subcontractor need to call your soil treatment company (exterminator) to have the soil treated against termites. The foundation should then be waterproofed, although this step can be done later. Your lender will require a foundation survey to show that the house is not in violation of any setbacks, and is of the dimensions indicated on your plans. You should call your surveyor to request this survey immediately after the foundation is completed, because you won't be able to receive any construction funds until your lender has a copy of the survey and a copy of your Builder's Risk insurance policy.

7. Plumbing rough-in, for slabs. Prior to pouring concrete, your plumber will install any pipes that will be under the slab. His work needs to be inspected prior to pouring the concrete. Any electrical conduits need to be installed also and inspected prior to pouring. If you don't have inspectors for these two items in your area, hire a professional.

8. Slabs. Concrete slabs need to be inspected prior to the concrete being poured, but after completing #7. This inspection is to assure that the slab will comply with codes. Most codes require the following: proper packing down of fill dirt, called tamping; 4–6 inches of sand or gravel for drainage; wire mesh; polyurethane (poly); a border of styrofoam for insulation; a uniform thickness of the slab throughout; and treatment of the soil. Also, the places where the load bearing walls or posts will rest need to have the slab thickened in accordance to code, usually the same thickness as the footing. A good concrete subcontractor will do all this, even ordering the soil treatment. If you don't have local inspectors for this step, hire a professional.

9. Kit erection and drying in. As mentioned in Chapter 8, it is best if you find a carpenter who has built a log home before, preferably one of the kind you are building. Construction manuals or guides that instruct your carpenter as to kit erection are usually available from the manufacturer. If any questions come up, your log home company can answer them and, in some cases, send an expert out on the job if the need arises. Drying in is the stage of construction where your house is protected from rain or snow. It doesn't mean that the roof shingles are on, but it can. If not roof shigles, building paper (felt) will protect the interior. Exterior trim of the FACIA, SOFFIT, and GABLE ends should be included in your contract with your carpenter and can be completed at this time.

10. Chimney and fireplace(s). Prior to installation of roofing shingles, fireplaces and chimneys should be built or installed. By finishing this step before roofing, proper FLASHING can be installed around the chimney. It also prevents damage to the shingles

American Lincoln Homes takes the cozy comfort of log home living to new heights. These beautiful, roomy duplex condominiums are presently being built on the North Carolina coast. American Lincoln offers a complete line of energy-efficient home packages in a choice of cedar, cypress, or Eastern white pine. (Courtesy American Lincoln Homes)

to have this step completed first.

11. Roofing. Roof shingles can be installed earlier, but it is best to wait. If done before chimneys, the roofer should leave a sufficient area around where any masonry chimney is to be built. The roofer will then have to come back later to finish. If so, only pay for the SQUARES installed, and possibly hold back ten percent of that.

12. Plumbing, HVAC, and electrical rough-ins. Usually the electrician waits until the plumbing and HVAC are roughed in before he starts work. This lessens the chance of having his wires cut accidentally. If your blueprints don't have an electrical plan, and many don't, he will go through the house with you and mark where you want switches, special receptacles (outlets), lights, or any other special wiring. The same is true for the HVAC. You don't want heat vents where you plan to place a piece of furniture. Plumbing is usually done in strict accordance with your plans, but your plumber may want to go through the house with you before he begins to be sure you understand and agree with the plans and specifications. This is wise, as things may look different in reality. Tubs and molded showers are installed during rough-in. With all three subcontractors, you can meet at your convenience, i.e. lunch hours, after work, or weekends. All three rough-ins require inspections.

13. Insulation. Even though your walls don't need insulation, the rest of your house does. Now is the time for it. It should be inspected for compliance with local codes, and/or utility company codes. If you don't have a local inspector, often the utility company does. Inspection of insulation checks for proper installation, proper material and thickness, proper VAPOR BARRIERS, and packing of spaces and cracks around windows and doors, etc.

14. Hardwood flooring and carpet underlayment. This step can be done after #15, but it is easier to do now. NOTE: if your subfloor is ¾-inch tongue and groove plywood, you won't need carpet underlayment.

15. Drywall and/or paneling. In areas that will have moisture, you may want to use waterproof sheetrock.

16. Interior trim. Doors, modlings, cabinets, bookcases, etc., are now ready to be installed.

17. Painting and staining. Your painter can do the exterior staining after #9, but he may want to wait and do the whole job at one time. Discuss this with him. If you wait too long for the outside work, you could have uneven fading, excessive CHECKING, mold, etc. Of course, if you are merely going to treat the wood and let it age or "weather," outside staining won't be your concern. You might want, however, to stain the exterior with a weathering stain that promotes even weathering. This would also provide protection to your wood.

18. Tile, counter tops, etc. At this time, counter tops and bath floors must be finished so that the plumbing can be completed. Kitchen floors also are finished at this point. You can also wallpaper at this time, unless you want to wait for either final selection of color and design, or to see how the cost of the house is coming out.

19. Trim out plumbing. Also called "setting the fixtures." At this time, your plumber will install sinks, commodes, water heater, faucets, dishwasher and disposal (but not the wiring of these appliances), and any other plumbing fixtures called for in your plans and specs. He needs to preceed your electrician. A final plumbing inspection is necessary.

20. Trim out HVAC. At this time the heating and air system is finished and inspected. This also needs to be completed before your electrician finishes his wiring of the house.

21. Trim out electrical. The electrician will install switches, receptacles, and Circuit Breakers. He will also wire the appliances installed by the plumber, as well as the furnace(s) and AC units. He will also install and wire electric ovens and ranges and any other electrical appliances or devices according to your plans and specs. He will also wire and hang all light fixtures, including doorbells, etc. A final electrical inspection is necessary.

22. Floor finish and/or carpet. Have floors finished before carpet. You may want to protect all floors when done with red waxed paper available at most building supply companies.

23. Clean up. You can do some or all of this, but doing windows can be dangerous, if you have to get on a ladder.

24. Drives and walks. This step can be done earlier, but heavy trucks can cause damage.

25. Landscaping. Most lenders require landscaping to be completed before they will close the permanent loan. This can be difficult at certain times of the year, so you may want to start on it as early as possible.

26. Final inspections. Besides the inspections already mentioned, you may be required to have a final building inspection. This inspection is to assure the safety of the house (i.e., handrails where required on stairs, etc.). It also is to be sure that everyting meets local and state codes. Your lenders, both construction and permanent, will make a final inspection. If you don't have a local building inspector, for your own peace of mind, hire a professional.

27. Loan closing. This can be arranged to be at a convenient time for you. Your attorney will prepare all the paperwork and inform you if you need to obtain any Lien

WAIVERS or other documents, such as your necessary homeowners insurance policy. If you do, be sure he tells you a few days in advance. As defined in the Glossary, a lien waiver merely proves that any materials or labor have been paid for.

28. ENJOY FOR A LIFETIME!

This is the "Cedardale" model from Cedardale Homes, Inc. Dormer windows, stone chimney and foundation covering, large front porch, roof overhangs, and garage add to the beauty of this energy-efficient log home. This was the featured home at the 1983 Cleveland Home Show as well as the 1984 Atlanta Home Show. (Courtesy Cedardale Homes, Inc.)

CHAPTER 11
Useful Tips That Save

Buying Land

• Seldom is the asking price for land the same as the selling price. Remember that when you are buying your land as it could save you a lot of money. Most sellers have a real estate commission built into their asking price as well as a cushion to negotiate. If you are not using a broker, you should ask for at least the amount a broker would earn as a discount. Then try to get the price down further still. Nothing ventured, nothing gained. It's a game, sometimes maddening perhaps, but it's the only game I know of where there can be two winners.

• Before making a final decision on purchasing your land, have your surveyor determine if your home can be situated so that your sewer or septic system will have a gravity flow and not require a lift station or pump. He most likely will have to call in either city sanitation engineers or health officials, or engineers, (for septic system location), but let him handle it. Avoiding a lift station is wise. They are expensive, and if they break down or the power goes out, you'll have a problem.

• Also, be sure there will be adequate drainage of surface water, or "runoff" away from your house. Your surveyor can determine this quite easily. Natural grades can usually be changed to accomplish this, but not always. Changing grades may involve the need for a higher and more costly foundation. Also, fill dirt and/or more grading will increase costs. Water problems can be avoided more easily than they can be remedied. Builders have a healthy respect for water. You will, too, if you consider the Grand Canyon.

• If your house is to be built on a crawl space or slab, try to select land or a lot with a relatively flat building site. This will cut down on foundation costs.

• Wooded land usually has a higher resale value. It is also usually easier to landscape and maintain landscaping by leaving most areas "natural."

Planning

• A time of high interest rates can create a slow down in construction. Don't let it slow you down, for it also usually means lower prices and better availability from subcontractors and suppliers.

• Review your plans very carefully during the planning stage. Try to make any and all changes before you even get estimates. Changes later on, especially in the building stage, are very expensive. In my estimation, changes are one of the most significant causes of cost overruns, as well as misunderstandings with suppliers and subcontractors.

• Every reduction in square footage you can make will reduce construction costs.

• Keep roof design simple and roof pitch moderate in order to keep costs down. The higher the pitch, the more valleys and ridges, the higher the cost.

• Laundry rooms can be located right outside bedroom areas (where most of the dirty laundry accumulates) even in two story houses. A floor drain should be provided in case of a leak or overflow. In some cases, this move will lower plumbing cost by closer grouping of plumbing (closer to the baths), therefore using less material to plumb. The convenience of having laundry rooms near bedrooms should be obvious.

Financing

• Try to shop for money as you would any product. A ½% point in interest or closing costs is a lot of money. You can do it over the phone on your lunch hour. Try to get loans with those lenders that offer the best rates.

Suppliers

• Some of the items that you may select to go into your house may not be stocked by

This American Log Home is a contemporary custom design, located near San Antonio, Texas. It features exposed beam ceilings, balcony, clearstory windows, and French doors. American features double tongue and groove logs with a protective drip edge. (Courtesy American Log Homes)

local suppliers, and may take weeks, or even months, to get. Very typical of this situation are plumbing fixtures, lighting fixtures, and other specialty items. Shop early and order early to avoid delays. Keep the job moving and you'll keep the cost of construction interest down.

• On the same subject, don't spend too much time and energy (or money) worrying about the small things that will go into your house. I've seen people agonize over decisions as to doorknobs, faucets, et cetera, only to forget what they look like a few months after their house was completed.

Building

• If you encounter any difficulties in obtaining permits from building inspection agencies, due to their unfamiliarity with log homes, contact your log home manufacturer or representative. It is wise to contact the inspection agency when you first start thinking of building a log home. Energy efficiency is the item usually unfamiliar to these agencies. Your log home representative or the publication, "The Energy Economics and Thermal Performance of Log Homes," Muir Publishing Co., Ltd. (see recommended reading list) should provide sufficient information to educate them.

• I have found a brick mason subcontractor that stakes the house, digs and pours the footing, installs the batter boards, and lays the foundation. The cost is about the same as using separate subs for each function, but the time to complete the foundation stage is lessened due to having to schedule only one sub. It also saves me time for the same reason. I do have my surveyor check for accuracy.

• After clearing your lot, you may want your clearing and excavation sub to spread unwashed crushed stone on your driveway. This will provide a hard surface that will allow access to your job site in wet weather, preventing delays in deliveries.

• When clearing a wooded lot, either give the wood to your sub in return for a lower contract price, or have him leave it in long lengths out of the way of the job site for you to cut at your leisure. Don't have him include cutting it into fireplace lengths unless you are willing to pay dearly for it.

• Be sure to have your plumber protect water lines from freezing. It will save you much aggravation and money in the dead of a hard winter. Try to have water lines plumbed into interior walls, and well protected in crawl spaces. Usually, in a log home, pipes are plumbed into interior walls due to the difficulty of plumbing them through the logs. But, watch for non-log walls such as dormers, garages, attic areas and the like. Wells should also be protected. Consult with your plumber on all of the above.

• Insulation in non-log walls, as well as gables, crawl spaces and, most importantly, attics and roofs, should be kept as free of moisture as possible. Insulation loses its effectiveness, often dramatically, when it contains moisture. This results in higher energy bills for you. Good ventilation in attic areas, roofs and crawl spaces and a moisture barrier in stud walls will aid in keeping moisture at a minimum in the insulation. Keep attic vents open in the winter. Crawl space vents, due to the prospect of having water lines freezing, unfortunately, can't be left open.

• In a house with upstairs plumbing, I recommend cast iron drain lines between the first and second levels. This cuts down on noise considerably. The rest of the drains can be PVC to cut costs. Be sure this is indicated in your specs.

• Interior bathroom walls can be insulated to cut noise. It's not too expensive.

• You may be able to get a lower price from your painting subcontractor if he is allowed to prime coat any interior walls that are to be painted before your carpenters install the interior trim. This is especially true if the interior trim is to be stained. If he can stain the trim before it is installed, a further savings might be realized.

• For log homes requiring chinking, new materials have revolutionized the chinking process. The materials used look like traditional mortar chinking, but while maintaining a strong adhesive bond, they remain flexible. Since a log home is subject to shrinkage and movement, as is any home, in the past chinking would crack and fall out. But with the new materials, the chinking stays in place. Two companies that market these new materials are Perma-Chink and Weatherall.

This American Log Home is the "Forester" model which is 28' x 40' with full first and second floors. Total square footage of this popular model is over 2200 square feet. American Log Homes uses Engelmann spruce, lodgepole pine, Douglas fir, and Southern yellow pine in various parts of its homes. (Courtesy American Log Homes)

APPENDIX

MANAGER'S CONSTRUCTION CONTRACT

1. General

This contract dated _____ is between _____
_____(OWNER) and
_____(MANAGER),
and provides for supervision of construction by MANAGER of a Log Home to be built on OWNER'S
Property at _____, and de-
scribed as _____.
The project is described on plans dated _____ and specifictions dated
_____, which documents are a part hereof.

2. Schedule

The project is to start as near as possible to _____, with anticipated completion
_____ months from starting date.

3. Contract Fee and Payment

3A. OWNER agrees to pay MANAGER a mimimum fee of _____
($) for the work performed under this contract, said fee to be paid in installments as the
work progresses as follows:

a. Foundation complete	$ _____
b. Kit erected	$ _____
c. Dryed-in	$ _____
d. Ready for drywall	$ _____
e. Trimmed out	$ _____
f. Final	$ _____

3B. Payments billed by MANAGER are due in full within ten (10) days of bill mailing date.
3C. Final payment to MANAGER is due in full upon completion of residence; however, MANAGER
may bill upon "Substantial completion" (see paragraph 11.0 for the definition of terms) the amount
of the final payment less 10% of the value of work yet outstanding. In such a case, the amount of
the fee withheld will be billed upon completion.

4. General Intent of Contract

It is intended that the OWNER be in effect his own "General Contractor" and that the MANAGER
provide the OWNER with expert guidance and advice, and supervision and coordination of trades
and material delivery. It is agreed that MANAGER acts in a professional capacity and simply as
agent for OWNER, and that as such he shall not assume or incur any pecuniary responsibility to
contractor, subcontractors, laborers or material suppliers. OWNER will contract directly with subcontractors, obtain from them their certificates of insurance and release of liens. Similarly, OWNER will
open his own accounts with material suppliers and be billed and pay directly for materials supplied.
OWNER shall insure that insurance is provided toprotect all parties of interest. OWNER shall pay
all expenses incurred in completing the project, except MANAGER'S overhead as specifically
exempted in Paragraph 9. In fulfilling his responsibilities to OWNER, MANAGER shall perform at all
times in a manner intended to be beneficial to the interests of the OWNER.

5. Responsibilities of Manager

General

MANAGER shall have full responsibility for coordination of trades, ordering materials and scheduling
of work, correction of errors and conflicts, if any, in the work, materials, or plans, compliance with

applicable codes, judgement as to the adequacy of trades' work to meet standards specified, together with any other function that might reasonably be expected in order to provide OWNER with a single source of responsibility for supervision and coordination of work.

Specific Responsibilities

1) Submit to OWNER in a timely manner a list of subcontractors and suppliers MANAGER believes competent to perform the work at competitive prices. OWNER may use such recommendations or not at his option.

2) Submit to OWNER a list of items requiring OWNER'S selection, with schedule dates for selection indicated, and recommended sources indicated.

3) Obtain in OWNER'S name(s) all permits required by governmental authorities.

4) Arrange for all required surveys and site engineering work.

5) Arrange for all the installation of temporary services.

6) Arrange for and supervise clearing, disposal of stumps and brush, and all excavating and grading work.

7) Develop material lists and order all materials in a timely manner, from sources designated by OWNER.

8) Schedule, coordinate, and supervise the work for all subcontractors designated by OWNER.

9) Review, when requested by OWNER, questionable bills and recommend payment action to OWNER.

10) Arrange for common labor for hand digging, grading, and clean-up during construction, and for disposal of construction waste.

11.) Supervise the project through completion, as defined in Paragraph 11.

6. Responsibilities of Owner

OWNER agrees to:

1) Arrange all financing needed for project, so that sufficient funds exist to pay all bills within ten (10) days of their presentation.

2) Select subcontractors and suppliers in a timely manner so as not to delay the work. Establish charge accounts and execute contracts with same, as appropriate, and inform MANAGER of accounts opened and of MANAGER'S authority in using said accounts.

3) Select items requiring OWNER selection, and inform MANAGER of selections and sources on or before date shown on selection list.

4) Inform MANAGER promptly of any changes desired or other matters affecting schedule so that adjustments can be incorporated in the schedule.

5) Appoint an agent to pay for work and make decisions in OWNER'S behalf in cases where OWNER is unavailable to do so.

6) Assume complete responsibility for any theft and vandalism of OWNER'S property occurring on the job. Authorize replacement/repairs required in a timely manner.

7) Provide a surety bond for his lender if required.

8) Obtain release of liens documentation as required by OWNER'S lender.

9) Provide insurance coverage as listed in Paragraph 12.

10) Pay promptly for all work done, materials used, and other services and fees generated in the execution of the project, except as specifically exempted in Paragraph 9.

7. Exclusions

The following items shown on the drawings and/or specifications are NOT included in this contract, in-so-far as MANAGER supervision responsibilities are concerned:
(List below) _____

_____

_____

_____

_____

_____

_____

_____

_____

_____

8. Extras/Changes

MANAGER'S fee is based on supervising the project as defined in the drawings and specifications. Should additional supervisory work be required because of EXTRAS or CHANGES occasioned by OWNER, unforseen site conditions, or governmental authorities, MANAGER will be paid an additional fee of 15% of cost of such work. Since the basic contract fee is a *minimum fee*, no downward adjustment will be made if the scope of work is reduced, unless contract is cancelled in accordance with Paragraphs 14 or 15.

9. Manager's Facilities

MANAGER will furnish his own transportation and office facilities for MANAGER'S use in supervising the project at no expense to OWNER. MANAGER shall provide general liability and workmen's compensation insurance coverage for MANAGER'S direct employees only at no cost to OWNER.

10. Use of MANAGER'S Accounts

MANAGER may have certain "trade" accounts not available to OWNER which OWNER may find it to his advantage to utilize. If MANAGER is billed and pays such accounts from MANAGER'S resources, OWNER will reimburse MANAGER within ten (10) days of receipt of MANAGER'S bill at cost plus 8% of such materials/services.

11. Project Completion

1. The project shall be deemed completed when all the terms of this contract have been fulfilled, and a Residential Use Permit has been issued.

2. The project shall be deemed "substantially complete" when a Residential Use Permit has been issued, and less than Five Hundred Dollars ($500) of work remains to be done.

12. Insurance

OWNER shall insure that workmen's compensation and general liability insurance are provided to protect all parties of interest and shall hold MANAGER harmless from all claims by subcontractors, suppliers and their personnel, and for personnel arranged for by MANAGER in OWNER'S behalf, if any.

OWNER shall maintain fire and extended coverage insurance sufficient to provide 100% coverage of project value at all stages of construction, and MANAGER shall be named in the policy to insure his interest in the project.

Should OWNER or MANAGER determine that certain subcontractors, laborers, or suppliers are not adequately covered by general liability or workmen's compensation insurance to protect OWNER'S and/or MANAGER'S interests, MANAGER may as agent of OWNER, cover said personnel on MANAGER'S policies, and OWNER shall reimburse MANAGER for the premium at cost plus 10%.

13. Manager's Right to Terminate Contract

Should the work be stopped by any public authority for a period of 30 days or more through no fault of the MANAGER, or should work be stopped through act or neglect of OWNER for ten (10) days or more, or should OWNER fail to pay MANAGER any payment due within ten (10) days written notice to OWNER, MANAGER may stop work and/or terminate this contract and recover from OWNER payment for all work completed as a proration of the total contract sum, plus 25% of the fee remaining to be paid if the contract were completed as liquidated damages.

14. Owner's Right to Terminate Contract

Should the work be stopped or wrongly prosecuted through act or neglect of MANAGER for ten (10) days or more, OWNER may so notify MANAGER in writing. If work is not properly resumed within ten (10) days of such notice, OWNER may terminate this contract. Upon termination, entire balance then due MANAGER for that percentage of work then completed, as a proration of the total contract sum, shall be due and payable and all further liabilities of MANAGER under this contract shall cease. Balance due to MANAGER shall take into account any additional cost to OWNER to complete the house occasioned by MANAGER.

15. MANAGER/OWNER'S Liability For Collection Expenses

Should MANAGER or OWNER respectively be required to collect funds rightfully due him through legal proceedings, MANAGER or OWNER respectively agrees to pay all costs and reasonable Attorney's fees.

16. Warranties and Service

MANAGER warrants that he will supervise the construction in accordance with the terms of this contract. No other warranty by MANAGER is implied or exists.

Subcontractors normally warrant their work for one year, and some manufacturers supply yearly warranties on certain of their equipment; such warranties shall run to the OWNER and the enforcement of these warranties is in all cases the responsibility of the OWNER and not the MANAGER.

(MANAGER) _____(SEAL)   DATE: _____

(OWNER) _____(SEAL)   DATE: _____

(OWNER) _____(SEAL)   DATE: _____

FIXED PRICE CONTRACT

CONTRACTOR: _____

OWNER:_____DATE:_____

OWNER is or shall become fee simple owner of a tract or parcel of land known or described as: _____. CONTRACTOR hereby agrees to construct a Log Home on the above described lot according to the plans drawn by _____. and the specifications herein attached.

OWNER shall pay CONTRACTOR for the construction of said house $_____ .

Prior to commencement hereunder, owner shall secure financing for the construction of said house in the amount of $ _____, which loan shall be disbursed from time to time as construction progresses, subject to a holdback of no more than 10%. OWNER hereby authorizes CONTRACTOR to submit a request for draws in the name of the OWNER from the Savings and Loan, or similar institution, up to the percentage completion of construction and to accept said draws in partial payment hereof.

CONTRACTOR shall commence construction as soon as feasible after closing and shall pursue work to a scheduled completion on or before 7 months from commencement, except if such completion shall be delayed by unusually unfavorable weather, strikes, natural disasters, unavailability of labor or materials, or changes in the plans and specifications.

CONTRACTOR shall build the residence in substantial compliance with the plans and specifications and in a good workmanlike manner, and shall meet all building code requirements. CONTRACTOR shall not be responsible for failure of materials or equipment not CONTRACTOR'S fault. Except as herein set out, CONTRACTOR shall make no representations or warranties with respect to the work to be done hereunder.

OWNER shall not occupy the residence and CONTRACTOR shall hold the keys until all work has been completed and all monies due CONTRACTOR hereunder have been paid.

OWNER shall not make any changes to the plans and specifications until such changes shall be evidenced in writing, the costs, if any, of such changes shall be set out, and any additional costs thereof shall be paid in advance of the work being accomplished.

CONTRACTOR shall not be obligated to continue work hereunder in the event OWNER shall breach any term or condition hereof, or if for any reason construction draws shall cease to be advanced upon proper request thereof.

Any additional or special stipulations attached hereto and signed by the parties shall be and are made a part hereof.

CONTRACTOR:_____(SEAL)

OWNER: _____(SEAL)

_____(SEAL)

FIXED FEE CONTRACT

CONTRACTOR:_____

OWNER:_____ DATE:_____

OWNER is or shall become fee simple owner of a tract or parcel of land known or described as; _____. CONTRACTOR hereby agrees to construct a Log Home on the above described lot according to the plans and specifications identified as: Exhibit A—plans and specifications drawn _____by _____.

OWNER shall pay CONTRACTOR for the construction of said house cost of construction and a fee of _____. Cost is estimated in Exhibit B. Each item in Exhibit B is an estimate and is not to be construed as an exact cost.

OWNER shall secure/has secured financing for the construction of said house in the amount of cost + fee, which shall be disbursed by a Savings and Loan or Bank from time to time as construction progresses, subject to a holdback of no more than 10%. OWNER hereby authorizes CONTRACTOR to submit a request for draws in the name of OWNER under such loan up to the percentage completion of construction and to accept said draws in partial payment hereof. In addition, it is understood that the CONTRACTOR'S fee shall be paid in installments by the Savings and Loan or Bank at the time of and as a part of each construction draw as a percentage of completion, so that the entire fee shall be paid at or before the final construction draw.

CONTRACTOR shall commence construction as soon as feasible after closing of the construction loan and shall pursue work to a scheduled completion on or before 7 months from commencement, except if such completion shall be delayed by unusually unfavorable weather, strikes, natural disasters, unavailability of labor or materials, or changes in the plans or specifications.

CONTRACTOR shall build the residence in substantial compliance with the plans and specifications and in a good and workmanlike manner, and shall meet all building codes. Contractor shall not be responsible for failure of materials or equipment not CONTRACTOR'S fault. Except as herein set out, Contractor shall make no representations or warranties with respect to the work to be done hereunder. OWNER shall not occupy the residence and CONTRACTOR shall hold the keys until all work has been completed and all monies due CONTRACTOR hereunder shall have been paid.

OWNER shall not make changes to the plans or specifications until such changes shall be evidenced in writing, the costs, if any, of such change shall be set out, and the construction lender and CONTRACTOR shall have approved such changes. Any additiional costs thereof shall be paid in advance, or payment guaranteed in advance of the work being accomplished.

CONTRACTOR shall not be obligated to continue work hereunder in the event OWNER shall breach any term or condition hereof, or if for any reason the construction lender shall cease making advances under the construction loan upon proper request thereof. Any additional or special stipulations attached hereto and signed by the parties shall be and are made a part hereof.

OWNER: _____(SEAL)

_____(SEAL)

CONTRACTOR: _____(SEAL)

CARPENTRY LABOR CONTRACT

TO: _____   SUB CONT. _____
(YOUR NAME)

_____   _____
(ADDRESS)

_____   _____

DATE:_____   JOB ADDRESS _____

                                       _____

OWNER:_____   _____

AREA: Heated   _____SQ. FT.

          Unheated   _____SQ. FT.

          Decks   _____SQ. FT.

CHARGES

Kit Erection   @_____Sq. Ft. x _____Sq. Ft. = $_____

Exterior Trim   @_____Sq. Ft. x _____Sq. Ft. = $_____

Interior Trim   @_____Sq. Ft. x _____Sq. Ft. = $_____

Decks   @_____Sq. Ft. x _____Sq. Ft. = $_____

Setting Fireplace $_____

Setting Cabinets   _____

Paneling   _____

Misc.   _____

                                          TOTAL CHARGES $_____

Terms of payment:_____

_____

Insurance Information:_____
                      NAME OF INSURED

_____
INSURANCE COMPANY   POLICY NUMBER

SIGNED:_____   DATE: _____
       (YOUR NAME)

SIGNED:_____   DATE: _____
       (SUBCONTRACTOR)

SUBCONTRACTOR'S INVOICE

Request Number: _____

TO: _____   CONTRACTOR: _____

_____   _____

_____   _____

DATE: _____   CONTRACT NUMBER: _____

CHANGE ORDER NUMBER: _____

WORKMENS COMP. INS. CO.: _____

JOB NAME	JOB NO.	DESCRIPTION OF WORK	AMOUNT

Work Completed in Accordance with Contract: Total:

LESS RETAINAGE:

_____

(Contractor)

NET AMOUNT DUE:

FHA Form 2005
VA Form 26-1852
Rev. 2/74

For accurate register of carbon copies, form
may be separated along above fold. Staple
completed sheets together in original order.

Form Approved
OMB No. 63–RO055

DESCRIPTION OF MATERIALS

No. _____
(To be inserted by FHA or VA)

☐ Proposed Construction

☐ Under Construction

Property address _____ City _____ State _____

Mortgagor or Sponsor _____ _____
(Name)   (Address)

Contractor or Builder _____ _____
(Name)   (Address)

INSTRUCTIONS

1. For additional information on how this form is to be submitted, number of copies, etc., see the instructions applicable to the FHA Application for Mortgage Insurance or VA Request for Determination of Reasonable Value, as the case may be.

2. Describe all materials and equipment to be used, whether or not shown on the drawings, by marking an X in each appropriate check-box and entering the information called for in each space. If space is inadequate, enter "See misc." and describe under item 27 or on an attached sheet. THE USE OF PAINT CONTAINING MORE THAN FIVE-TENTHS OF ONE PERCENT LEAD BY WEIGHT IS PROHIBITED.

3. Work not specifically described or shown will not be considered unless required, then the minimum acceptable will be assumed. Work exceeding minimum requirements cannot be considered unless specifically described.

4. Include no alternates, "or equal" phrases, or contradictory items. (Consideration of a request for acceptance of substitute materials or equipment is not thereby precluded.)

5. Include signatures required at the end of this form.

6. The construction shall be completed in compliance with the related drawings and specifications, as amended during processing. The specifications include this Description of Materials and applicable Minimum Property Standards.

1. EXCAVATION:

Bearing soil, type _____

2. FOUNDATIONS:

Footings: concrete mix _____; strength psi _____ Reinforcing _____

Foundation wall: material _____ Reinforcing _____

Interior foundation wall: material _____ Party foundation wall _____

Columns: material and sizes _____ Piers: material and reinforcing _____

Girders: material and sizes _____ Sills: material _____

Basement entrance areaway _____ Window areaways _____

Waterproofing _____ Footing drains _____

Termite protection _____

Basementless space: ground cover _____; insulation _____; foundation vents _____

Special foundations _____

Additional information: _____

3. CHIMNEYS:

Material _____ Prefabricated (make and size) _____

Flue lining: material _____ Heater flue size _____ Fireplace flue size _____

Vents (material and size): gas or oil heater _____; water heater _____

Additional information: _____

4. FIREPLACES:

Type: ☐ solid fuel; ☐ gas-burning; ☐ circulator (make and size) _____ Ash dump and clean-out _____

Fireplace: facing _____; lining _____; hearth _____; mantel _____

Additional information: _____

5. EXTERIOR WALLS:

Wood frame: wood grade, and species _____ ☐ Corner bracing. Building paper or felt _____

Sheathing _____; thickness _____; width _____; ☐ solid; ☐ spaced _____" o. c.; ☐ diagonal; _____

Siding _____; grade _____; type _____; size _____; exposure _____"; fastening _____

Shingles _____; grade _____; type _____; size _____; exposure _____"; fastening _____

Stucco _____; thickness _____"; Lath _____; weight _____ lb.

Masonry veneer _____ Sills _____ Lintels _____ Base flashing _____

Masonry: ☐ solid ☐ faced ☐ stuccoed; total wall thickness _____"; facing thickness _____"; facing material _____

Backup material _____; thickness _____"; bonding _____

Door sills _____ Window sills _____ Lintels _____ Base flashing _____

Interior surfaces: dampproofing, _____ coats of _____; furring _____

Additional information: _____

Exterior painting: material _____; number of coats _____

Gable wall construction: ☐ same as main walls; ☐ other construction _____

6. FLOOR FRAMING:

Joists: wood, grade, and species _____ ; other _____ ; bridging _____ ; anchors _____

Concrete slab: ☐ basement floor; ☐ first floor; ☐ ground supported; ☐ self-supporting; mix _____ ; thickness _____ ";

  reinforcing _____ ; insulation _____ ; membrane _____

Fill under slab: material _____ ; thickness _____ ". Additional information: _____

_____

7. SUBFLOORING: *(Describe underflooring for special floors under item 21.)*

Material: grade nd species _____ ; size _____ ; type _____

Laid: ☐ first floor; ☐ second floor; ☐ attic _____ sq. ft.; ☐ diagonal; ☐ right angles. Additional information: _____

_____

8. FINISH FLOORING: *(Wood only.   Describe other finish flooring under item 21.)*

LOCATION	ROOMS	GRADE	SPECIES	THICKNESS	WIDTH	BLDG. PAPER	FINISH
First floor ____							
Second floor ____							
Attic floor ____ sq. ft.							

Additional information: _____

9. PARTITION FRAMING:

Studs: wood, grade, and species _____ size and spacing _____ Other _____

Additional information: _____

10. CEILING FRAMING:

Joists: wood, grade, and species _____ Other _____ Bridging _____

Additional information: _____

11. ROOF FRAMING:

Rafters: wood, grade, and species _____ Roof trusses (see detail): grade and species _____

Additional information: _____

12. ROOFING:

Sheathing: wood, grade, and species _____ ; ☐ solid; ☐ spaced _____ " o.c.

Roofing _____ ; grade _____ ; size _____ ; type _____

Underlay _____ ; weight or thickness _____ ; size _____ ; fastening _____

Built-up roofing _____ ; number of plies _____ ; surfacing material _____

Flashing: material _____ ; gage or weight _____ ; ☐ gravel stops; ☐ snow guards

Additional information: _____

13. GUTTERS AND DOWNSPOUTS:

Gutters: material _____ ; gage or weight _____ ; size _____ ; shape _____

Downspouts: material _____ ; gage or weight _____ ; size _____ ; shape _____ ; number _____

Downspouts connected to: ☐ Storm sewer; ☐ sanitary sewer; ☐ dry-well.   ☐ Splash blocks: material and size _____

Additional information: _____

14. LATH AND PLASTER

Lath ☐ walls, ☐ ceilings: material _____ ; weight or thickness _____ Plaster: coats _____ ; finish _____

Dry-wall ☐ walls, ☐ ceilings: material _____ ; thickness _____ ; finish _____ ;

Joint treatment _____

15. DECORATING: *(Paint, wallpaper, etc.)*

ROOMS	WALL FINISH MATERIAL AND APPLICATION	CEILING FINISH MATERIAL AND APPLICATION
Kitchen ____		
Bath ____		
Other ____		

Additional information: _____

16. INTERIOR DOORS AND TRIM:

Doors: type _____ ; material _____ ; thickness _____

Door trim: type _____ ; material _____ Base: type _____ ; material _____ ; size _____

Finish: doors _____ ; trim _____

Other trim *(item, type and location)* _____

Additional information: _____

7. WINDOWS:

Windows: type _____ ; make _____ ; material _____ ; sash thickness _____

Glass: grade _____ ; ☐ sash weights; ☐ balances, type _____ ; head flashing _____

Trim: type _____ ; material _____ Paint _____ ; number coats _____

Weatherstripping: type _____ ; material _____ Storm sash, number _____

Screens: ☐ full; ☐ half; type _____ ; number _____ ; screen cloth material _____

Basement windows: type _____ ; material _____ ; screens, number _____ ; Storm sash, number _____

Special windows _____

Additional information: _____

8. ENTRANCES AND EXTERIOR DETAIL:

Main entrance door: material _____ ; width _____ ; thickness _____". Frame: material _____ ; thickness _____"

Other entrance doors: material _____ ; width _____ ; thickness _____". Frame: material _____ ; thickness _____"

Head flashing _____ Weatherstripping: type _____ ; saddles _____

Screen doors: thickness _____"; number _____ ; screen cloth material _____ Storm doors: thickness _____"; number _____

Combination storm and screen doors: thickness _____"; number _____ ; screen cloth material _____

Shutters: ☐ hinged; ☐ fixed. Railings _____ , Attic louvers _____

Exterior millwork: grade and species _____ Paint _____ ; number coats _____

Additional information: _____

9. CABINETS AND INTERIOR DETAIL:

Kitchen cabinets, wall units: material _____ ; lineal feet of shelves _____ ; shelf width _____

Base units: material _____ ; counter top _____ ; edging _____

Back and end splash _____ Finish of cabinets _____ ; number coats _____

Medicine cabinets: make _____ ; model _____

Other cabinets and built-in furniture _____

Additional information: _____

10. STAIRS:

STAIR	TREADS		RISERS		STRINGS		HANDRAIL		BALUSTERS	
	Material	Thickness	Material	Thickness	Material	Size	Material	Size	Material	Size
Basement										
Main										
Attic										

Disappearing: make and model number _____

Additional information: _____

11. SPECIAL FLOORS AND WAINSCO

	LOCATION	MATERIAL, COLOR, BORDER, SIZES, GAGE, ETC.	THRESHOLD MATERIAL	WALL BASE MATERIAL	UNDERFLOOR MATERIAL
FLOORS	Kitchen				
	Bath				

	LOCATION	MATERIAL, COLOR, BORDER, CAP. SIZES, GAGE, ETC.	HEIGHT	HEIGHT OVER TUB	HEIGHT IN SHOWERS (FROM FLOOR)
WAINSCOT	Bath				

Bathroom accessories: ☐ Recessed; material _____ ; number _____ ; ☐ Attached; material _____ ; number _____

Additional information: _____

22. PLUMBING:

Fixture	Number	Location	Make	Mfr's Fixture Identification No.	Size	Color
Sink						
Lavatory						
Water closet						
Bathtub						
Shower over tub △						
Stall shower △						
Laundry trays						

△☐ Curtain rod   △☐ Door   ☐ Shower pan: material _____

Water supply: ☐ public; ☐ community system; ☐ individual (private) system. ★

Sewage disposal: ☐ public; ☐ community system; ☐ individual (private) system. ★

★ *Show and describe individual system in complete detail in separate drawings and specifications according to requirements.*

House drain (inside): ☐ cast iron; ☐ tile; ☐ other _____ House sewer (outside): ☐ cast iron; ☐ tile; ☐ other _____

Water piping: ☐ galvanized steel; ☐ copper tubing; ☐ other _____ Sill cocks, number _____

Domestic water heater: type _____; make and model _____; heating capacity _____ _____ gph. 100° rise. Storage tank: material _____; capacity _____ gallons.

Gas service: ☐ utility company; ☐ liq. pet. gas; ☐ other _____ Gas piping: ☐ cooking; ☐ house heating.

Footing drains connected to: ☐ storm sewer; ☐ sanitary sewer; ☐ dry well. Sump pump; make and model _____ _____; capacity _____; discharges into _____

23. HEATING:

☐ Hot water. ☐ Steam. ☐ Vapor. ☐ One-pipe system. ☐ Two-pipe system.

☐ Radiators. ☐ Convectors. ☐ Baseboard radiation. Make and model _____

Radiant panel: ☐ floor; ☐ wall; ☐ ceiling. Panel coil: material _____

☐ Circulator. ☐ Return pump. Make and model _____; capacity _____ gpm.

Boiler: make and model _____ Output _____ Btuh.; net rating _____ Btuh.

Additional information: _____

Warm air: ☐ Gravity. ☐ Forced. Type of system _____

Duct material: supply _____; return _____ Insulation _____, thickness _____ ☐ Outside air intake.

Furnace: make and model _____ Input _____ Btuh.; output _____ Btuh.

Additional information: _____

☐ Space heater; ☐ floor furnace; ☐ wall heater. Input _____ Btuh.; output _____ Btuh.; number units _____

Make, model _____ Additional information: _____

Controls: make and types _____

Additional information: _____

Fuel: ☐ Coal; ☐ oil; ☐ gas; ☐ liq. pet. gas; ☐ electric; ☐ other _____; storage capacity _____

Additional information: _____

Firing equipment furnished separately: ☐ Gas burner, conversion type. ☐ Stoker: hopper feed ☐; bin feed ☐

Oil burner: ☐ pressure atomizing; ☐ vaporizing _____

Make and model _____ Control _____

Additional information: _____

Electric heating system: type _____ Input _____ watts; @ _____ volts; output _____ Btuh.

Additional information: _____

Ventilating equipment: attic fan, make and model _____; capacity _____ cfm.

kitchen exhaust fan, make and model _____

Other heating, ventilating, or cooling equipment _____

24. ELECTRIC WIRING:

Service: ☐ overhead; ☐ underground. Panel: ☐ fuse box; ☐ circuit-breaker; make _____ AMP's _____ No. circuits _____

Wiring: ☐ conduit; ☐ armored cable; ☐ nonmetallic cable; ☐ knob and tube; ☐ other _____

Special outlets: ☐ range; ☐ water heater; ☐ other _____

☐ Doorbell. ☐ Chimes. Push-button locations _____ Additional information: _____

25. LIGHTING FIXTURES:

Total number of fixtures_____ Total allowance for fixtures, typical installation, $_____

Nontypical installation _____

Additional information: _____

26. INSULATION:

LOCATION	THICKNESS	MATERIAL, TYPE, AND METHOD OF INSTALLATION	VAPOR BARRIER
Roof			
Ceiling			
Wall			
Floor			

HARDWARE: *(make, material, and finish.)* _____

_____

SPECIAL EQUIPMENT: *(State material or make, model and quantity. Include only equipment and appliances which are acceptable by local law, custom and applicable FHA standards. Do not include items which, by established custom, are supplied by occupant and removed when he vacates premises or chattles prohibited by law from becoming realty.)*_____

_____
_____
_____
_____
_____
_____
_____

27. MISCELLANEOUS: *(Describe any main dwelling materials, equipment, or construction items not shown elsewhere; or use to provide additional information where the space provided was inadequate. Always reference by item number to correspond to numbering used on this form.)* _____

_____
_____
_____
_____
_____
_____
_____
_____

PORCHES:

_____
_____

TERRACES:

_____
_____

GARAGES:

_____
_____

WALKS AND DRIVEWAYS:

Driveway: width _____; base material _____; thickness _____"; surfacing material _____; thickness _____"

Front walk: width _____; material _____; thickness _____". Service walk: width _____; material _____; thickness _____"

Steps: material _____; treads _____"; risers _____". Cheek walls _____

OTHER ONSITE IMPROVEMENTS:

(Specify all exterior onsite improvements not described elsewhere, including items such as unusual grading, drainage structures, retaining walls, fence, railings, and accessóry structures.)

_____
_____
_____

LANDSCAPING, PLANTING, AND FINISH GRADING:

Topsoil_____" thick: ☐ front yard; ☐ side yards; ☐ rear yard to _____ feet behind main building.

Lawns *(seeded, sodded, or sprigged)*: ☐ front yard _____; ☐ side yards _____; ☐ rear yard_____.

Planting: ☐ as specified and shown on drawings; ☐ as follows:

_____ Shade trees, deciduous, _____" caliper.   _____ Evergreen trees. _____' to _____', B & B.

_____ Low flowering trees, deciduous, _____' to _____'   _____ Evergreen shrubs. _____' to _____', B & B.

_____ High-growing shrubs, deciduous, _____' to _____'   _____ Vines, 2-year _____

_____ Medium-growing shrubs, deciduous, _____' to _____'   _____

_____ Low-growing shrubs, deciduous, _____' to _____'   _____

IDENTIFICATION.—This exhibit shall be identified by the signature of the builder, or sponsor, and/or the proposed mortgagor if the latter is known at the time of application.

Date_____   Signature _____

                                            Signature _____

FHA Form 2005
VA Form 26–1852

Comparative Construction Cost Index*
for Major U.S. Cities
(New York City = 100%)

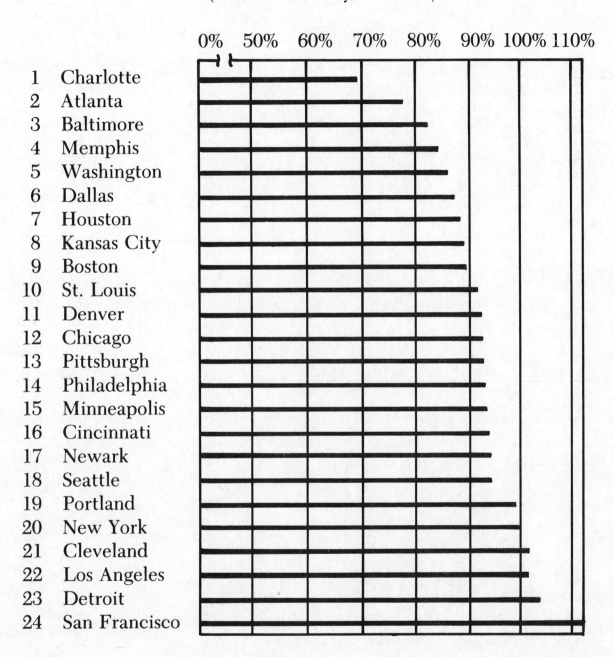

1	Charlotte
2	Atlanta
3	Baltimore
4	Memphis
5	Washington
6	Dallas
7	Houston
8	Kansas City
9	Boston
10	St. Louis
11	Denver
12	Chicago
13	Pittsburgh
14	Philadelphia
15	Minneapolis
16	Cincinnati
17	Newark
18	Seattle
19	Portland
20	New York
21	Cleveland
22	Los Angeles
23	Detroit
24	San Francisco

* Source: U.S. Construction Costs, Dodge Building Service, McGraw-Hill Information Systems Company, 1981

Savings and Loan Association

Inspection Report and Disbursement Schedule

DATE_____ Loan No. _____

Borrower_____

Location: Street/Box #_____ On_____ Side of_____

between _____and _____

in _____Subdivision _____County

ID by _____

Date Construction to Begin_____

Contractor _____Loan Officer _____

Date of Inspection

1. Start-up costs	1										
2. Rough clearing and grading	1										
3. Foundations	4										
4. Floor framing	4										
5. Wall framing	5										
6. Roof framing and sheeting	5										
7. Wall sheathing	1										
8. Roofing	2										
9. Well/water connection	2										
10. Septic tank/sewer tap	2										
11. Plumbing roughed	5										
12. Wiring roughed	3										
13. Heating-AC ducts	2										
14. Insulation	2										
15. Chimney/flue	2										
16. Siding/brick veneer	7										
17. Door frames set	2										
18. Windows set	3										
19. Particle board/flooring	2										
20. Inside walls	6										
21. Bath tile	2										
22. Outside trim	2										
23. Gutters	1										
24. Inside trim	3										
25. Doors hung	2										
26. Plumbing fixtures	4										
27. Cabinets	3										
28. Heat plant	2										
29. Exterior painting	2										
30. Interior painting	4										
31. Built-in-appliances	2										
32. Electrical fixtures	2										
33. Carpet/floor finish	4										
34. Screens	1										
35. Drives and walks	3										
36. Cleaning	1										
37. Landscaping	1										
TOTAL	100										
Date											
INSPECTOR											
INSPECTOR											

CERTIFICATE OF INSURANCE

ALLSTATE INSURANCE COMPANY   HOME OFFICE—NORTHBROOK, ILLINOIS

**Name and Address of Party to
Whom this Certificate is Issued**

Name and Address of Insured

INSURANCE
IN FORCE

TYPE OF INSURANCE AND HAZARDS	POLICY FORMS	LIMITS OF LIABILITY			POLICY NUMBER	EXPIRATION DATE
Workmen's Compensation **Employers' Liability**	STANDARD	STATUTORY * $ PER ACCIDENT (Employer's Liability only) *Applies only in following state(s):				
Automobile Liability		**Bodily Injury**	**Each**	**Property Damage**		
☐ OWNED ONLY	☐ BASIC	$	PERSON			
☐ NON-OWNED ONLY	☐ COMPRE-HENSIVE	$	ACCIDENT	$		
☐ HIRED ONLY	☐ GARAGE	$	OCCURRENCE	$		
☐ OWNED, NON-OWNED AND HIRED	☐	**Bodily Injury and Property Damage** (Single Limit) $ EACH ACCIDENT $ EACH OCCURRENCE				
General Liability		**Bodily Injury**		**Property Damage**		
☐ PREMISES—O.L.&T.	☐ SCHEDULE	$	EACH PERSON			
☐ OPERATIONS—M.&C.		$	EACH ACCIDENT	$		
☐ ELEVATOR	☐ COMPRE-HENSIVE	$	EACH OCCURRENCE	$		
☐ PRODUCTS/ COMPLETED OPERATIONS		$	AGGREG. PROD. COMP. OPTNS.	$		
☐ PROTECTIVE (Independent Contractors)	☐ SPECIAL MULTI-PERIL		AGGREGATE OPERATIONS	$		
☐ Endorsed to cover contract between insured and	☐		AGGREGATE PROTECTIVE	$		
			AGGREGATE CONTRACTUAL	$		
_____ _____ _____ dated_____		**Bodily Injury and Property Damage** (Single Limit) $ EACH ACCIDENT $ EACH OCCURRENCE $ AGGREGATE				

The policies identified above by number are in force on the date indicated below. With respect to a number entered under policy number, the type of insurance shown at its left is in force, but only with respect to such of the hazards, and under such policy forms, for which an "X" is entered, subject, however, to all the terms of the policy having reference thereto. The limits of liability for such insurance are only as shown above. This Certificate of Insurance neither affirmatively nor negatively amends, extends, nor alters the coverage afforded by the policy or policies numbered in this Certificate.

In the event of reduction of coverage or cancellation of said policies, the Allstate Insurance Company will make all reasonable effort to send notice of such reduction or cancellation to the certificate holder at the address shown above.

THIS CERTIFICATE IS ISSUED AS A MATTER OF INFORMATION ONLY AND CONFERS NO RIGHTS UPON THE CERTIFICATE HOLDER.

Date_____, 19____   By_____
                                                              Authorized Representative

U454-16
(6-75)

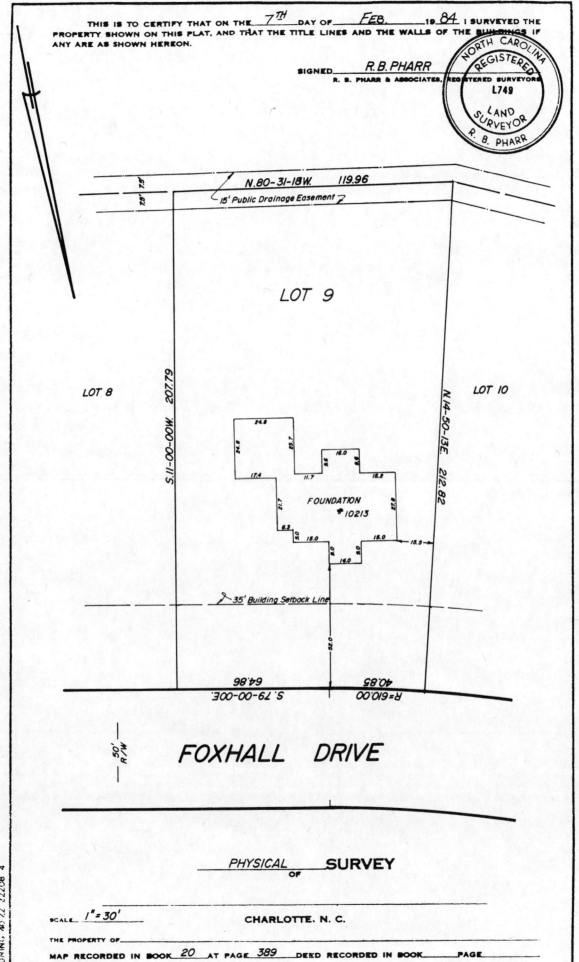

THIS IS TO CERTIFY THAT ON THE __7TH__ DAY OF __FEB.__ 19__84__ I SURVEYED THE PROPERTY SHOWN ON THIS PLAT, AND THAT THE TITLE LINES AND THE WALLS OF THE BUILDINGS IF ANY ARE AS SHOWN HEREON.

SIGNED ___R.B.PHARR___

R. B. PHARR & ASSOCIATES, REGISTERED SURVEYORS

NORTH CAROLINA
REGISTERED
L749
LAND
SURVEYOR
R. B. PHARR

N.80-31-18W. 119.96

15' Public Drainage Easement

LOT 9

LOT 8

S.11-00-00W. 207.79

LOT 10

N.14-50-13E. 212.82

24.8

24.8

23.7

16.0

9.6

9.6

17.4

11.7

15.2

21.7

FOUNDATION
#10213

22.8

6.3

5.0

18.0

18.0

18.5

8.0

8.0

14.0

52.0

35' Building Setback Line

64.86

S. 79-00-00 E.

40.85

R=610.00

50'
R/W

FOXHALL   DRIVE

PHYSICAL of SURVEY

SCALE __1"=30'__   CHARLOTTE, N.C.

THE PROPERTY OF _____

MAP RECORDED IN BOOK __20__ AT PAGE __389__   DEED RECORDED IN BOOK _____ PAGE _____

BRUNING 40 22 22208 4

Precut Log Home Manufacturers
Source: *Log Home Guide for Builders and Buyers*, Winter Directory

AAA Log Homes, Inc.
Box 94
Rayle, Georgia 30660
(404) 274-3201

Air-Lock Log Company, Inc.
P.O. Box 2506
Las Vegas, New Mexico 87701
(505) 425-8888

Alaska Log Homes & Lodges
P.O. Box 132
Carlton, Washington 98814
(509) 997-0080

Allegany Log Homes
Route 19
Houghton, NY 14744
(716) 567-2583

Alta Industries Ltd.
P.O. Box 88
Halcottsville, New York 12438
(914) 586-3336

American Heritage Log Homes
P.O. Box 216
Maggie Valley, North Carolina 28751
(704) 926-3411

American Lincoln Ltd.
P.O. Box 666
Battleboro, N.C. 27809
(919) 977-2545
800-682-8127 (NC)
800-334-5166 (US)

American Log Homes, Inc.
P.O. Box 7211
Pueblo West, Colorado 81007
(303) 547-2135

also:

P.O. Box 535
Bourbon, Missouri 65441
(314) 732-5206

American Tradition Log Homes, Inc.
P.O. Box 21246
Minneapolis, Minnesota 55421
(612) 571-6040

Appalachian Log Structures
Burke-Parsons-Bowlby Corporation
Dept. LHG, P.O. Box 86
Goshen, Virginia 24439
(703) 997-9251

Aspen Cabin Logs
Route 2
Frederic, Wisconsin 54837
(715) 653-2605

Authentic Homes Corp.
310 Grand Avenue
P.O. Box 1288
Laramie, Wyoming 82070
(307) 742-3786

Badger Country Log Homes, Inc.
P.O. Box 68
Waldo, Wisconsin 53093
(414) 458-4186

Barna & Danner Company
P.O. Box 538
Oneida, Tennessee 37841
(615) 569-8559
1-800-962-4734

Beaver Log Homes
A Division of Chisum Industries, Inc.
P.O. Box 1145
Claremore, Oklahoma 74018
(918) 341-5932

Bellaire Log Homes
P.O. Box 322
Bellaire, Michigan 49615
(616) 533-8633

Blue Ridge Cabins
Route 1
Wake Forest, North Carolina 25787
(919) 556-2391

Boyne Falls Log Homes, Inc.
Highway 131
Boyne Falls, Michigan 49713
(616) 549-2421

BRC Timberhomes
Route 1, Box 67
Wake Forest, North Carolina 27587
(919) 556-2391

Brentwood Log Homes, Inc.
94 East Main Street
Franklin, Tennessee 37064
(615) 790-9911

Lok Log Homes
A Division of Building Logs, Inc.
P.O. Box 300
Gunnison, Colorado 81230
(303) 641-1844

Cabin Log Company of America, Inc.
2809 Highway 167 North
Lafayette, Louisiana 70507
(318) 232-9568

Canadian Log Homes
P.O. Box 480
White Rock, South Carolina 29177
(803) 781-6070

Canadian Log Structures
R.R. 3, P.O. Box 9
Bobcaygeon, Ontario
KOM 1A0
(705) 738-4014

Cedardale Homes, Inc.
601 Friendship Center
Greensboro, North Carolina 27409
(919) 854-1752

Cedar River Log Homes, Inc.
325 S. Clinton St.
Grand Ledge, Michigan 48837
(517) 627-3676 or (517) 627-6123

Cee-Der Log Buildings
Division of L.K. Resources Ltd.
4100 6A Street N.E.
Calgary, Alberta T2A 4B1
(403) 277-8501/0167

Coley Dyalog Homes, Inc.
82 Wells Fargo
Austin, Texas 78737
(512) 288-3338

1867 Confederation Log Homes
Century Old Wood Products 1981
R.R. 3, P.O. Box 9
Bobcaygeon, Ontario KOM 1A0
(705) 738-4131

Country Best Log Homes
11816 Six Forks Road
Raleigh, North Carolina 27609
(919) 848-8350

Country Log Homes, Inc.
Route 7, P.O. Box 158
Ashley Falls, Massachusetts 01222
(413) 229-8084

Curries Log Building System Ltd.
Belmont, Colchester County
Nova Scotia B0M 1C0
(902) 662-2248

Eureka Log Homes, Inc.
Industrial Park
Berryville, Arkansas 72616
(501) 423-3396/97/98

Four Seasons Log Homes
TP Wood Products Limited
3425 Major McKenzie Drive
Woodbridge, Ontario L4L 1A6
(416) 832-2945

Gastineau Log Homes, Inc.
Highway 54
New Bloomfield, Missouri 65063
(314) 896-5611/4557

Gatlinburg Log Buildings
Great Smoky Mountains, Inc.
P.O. Box 145
Sevierville, Tennessee 37862
(615) 453-6770 or (615) 453-3331

Gold Hill Log Homes
Div. of Gold Hill Lumber Co, Inc.
P.O. Box 366
Gold Hill, North Carolina 28071
(704) 279-7850 or (704) 279-7715

Great Lakes Log Homes, Inc.
195 U.S. 31 South
Traverse City, Michigan 49684
(616) 943-4500

Greatwood Log Homes, Inc.
P.O. Box 707
Elkhart Lake, Wisconsin 53020
(414) 876-2357
800-558-5812 (US)
800-242-1021) (WI)

Green Mountain Log Homes
Green Mountain Cabins, Inc.
Box 190
Chester, Vermont 05143
(802) 875-2163

Green River Trading Company
P.O. Box 130, R.D. 2
Millerton, New York 12546
(518) 789-3311

Hayward Log Homes, Inc.
Highway 63 South, P.O. Box 794
Haward, Wisconsin 54843
(715) 634-3344/462-3722

Heritage Log Homes, Inc.
Box 610, Highway 73-E
Gatlinburg, Tennessee 37738
(615) 436-9331

Heritage Solid Wood Homes
1040 Redwood Highway
Mill Valley, California 94941
(415) 381-1151

Hiawatha Log Homes
P.O. Box 362
Marquette, Michigan 49855
(906) 343-6536

Holmes County Log Homes, Inc.
Box 220
Berlin, Ohio 44610
(216) 893-2255

Homestead Logs Limited
R.R. 2
King City, Ontario Log 1K0
(416) 727-4365

Honest Abe Log Homes
Rt #1, Box 84G
Moss, Tennessee 38575
(615) 258-3648

Joseph Log Homes
P.O. Box 727
Joseph, Oregon 97846
(503) 432-2311

Justus Cedar Homes
P.O. Box 98300
Tacoma, Washington 98499
(206) 582-3404

Katahdin Forest Products Co.
Box 145
Oakfield, Maine 04763
(207) 757-8278

Kentucky Log Homes, Inc.
P.O. Box 336, Highway 163 N.
Tompkinsville, Kentucky 42167
(502) 487-8798

KSM Enterprises Inc.
Star Route
McAlisterville, Pennsylvania 17049
(717) 463-2383/564-0885

Laurentien Log Homes Ltd.
5636 Route 117
Val-Morin, Quebec J0T 2R0
(514) 229-2933

Lengendary Log Homes
P.O. Box 845
Bobcaygeon, Ontario K0M 1A0
(705) 738-4264

Lincoln Log Homes
6000 Lumber Lane
Kannapolis, North Carolina 28081
(704) 932-6151

Lincoln Logs Ltd.
Box 135
Riverside Drive
Chestertown, N.Y. 12817
(518) 494-2426
800-833-2461

Lodge Logs by MacGregor
3200 Gowen Road
Boise, Idaho 83705
(208) 336-2450

Logcrafters, Inc.
P.O. Box 400
Cohutta, Georiga 30710
(404) 694-3302 or 800-241-4069

Log Homes of America, Inc.
P.O. Box 360107
Birmingham, Alabama 35236
800-225-LOGS

Log Structures of the South
Port of Sanford, P.O. Box 276
Lake Monroe, Florida 32747
(305) 831-5028 or (305) 321-LOGS

Lok-N-Logs
RD. No. 2, P.O. Box 212
Sherburne, New York 13460
(607) 674-4447

Maine Cedar Log Homes
L.C. Andrew, Inc.
933 Main Street
South Windham, Maine 04082
(207) 892-8561 or 1-800-341-0405

La Maison du Patriote
116 Boul. Des Laurentides
C.P. 428, Piedmont
Quebec J0R 1K0
(514) 227-3232 or (514) 227-6966

Maisons d'Autrefois du Quebec, Inc.
5500 Chemin Renaud, C.P. 55
Ste-Agathe des Monts
Quebec J8C 2Z8
(819) 326-6604

Model-Log
Lumber Enterprises, Inc.
75777 Gallatin Road
Bozeman, Montana 59715
(406) 763-4411

Mountaineer Log Homes, Inc.
Boot Road, P.O. Box 251
Downingtown, Pennsylvania 19335
(215) 873-0140

Mountaineer Log & Siding Co.
Star Route 1, Box 42
(U.S. Route 219 North)
Oakland, Maryland 21550
(301) 334-9772

Mountain Gem Log Homes
219 Dover Highway, Suite 21
Sandpoint, Idaho 83841
(208) 263-3867

National Log Construction Co.
Box 7458
Missoula, Montana 59807
(406) 728-6823

Box 69
Thompson Falls, Montana 59873
(406) 827-3522

Natural Log Homes, Inc
Route 2, Box 164
Noel, Missouri 64854
(417) 475-3183

Neville's Log Homes
A Division of Nevilog, Inc.
West Fork Route
Darby, Montana 59829
(406) 821-3921

New England Log Homes, Inc.
2301 State Street, P.O. Box 5056
Hamden, Connecticut 06518
(203) 562-9981
800-243-3551

New Homestead Log Company
Box 161, Lot 4
Payette, Idaho 83661
(515) 782-2890 or (208) 642-2883

North Country Log Homes
Devon Mills Lts.
P.O. Box 1180
Chapleau, Ontario P0M 1K0
(705) 864-1190

Northeastern Log Homes, Inc.
Box 126
Groton, Vermont 05046
(802) 584-3336

Northern Log Homes
Log Systems of Canada Inc.
Site 6, Comp. 9, R.R. 1
Vernon, British Columbia V1T 6L4
(604) 549-4216

Original Log Cabins Ltd.
Box 239
Pine River, Manitoba R0L 1M0
(204) 263-5209 or (204) 734-2925

Otsego Cedar Log Homes
P.O. Box 147
Gaylord, MI 49735
(517) 732-6268

Pan-Abode Buildings Canada
20900 Westminster Highway
Richmond, British Columbia V6V 1V5
(604) 270-7891

Pan Abode Cedar Homes
4350 Lake Washington Blvd., North
Renton, Washington 98056
(206) 255-8260

Pinecraft Log Homes
2805 W. Breezewood Lane
Neenah, Wisconsin 54956
(414) 729-6132

Precision Log Homes
Route 1, Box 111
Poplar Bluff, Missouri 63901
(314) 785-5576/0700

Proctor Piper Log Homes, Inc.
RD. No. 1, Box 146
Proctorsville, Vermont 05153
(802) 226-7224

R & L Log Building, Inc.
Mt. Upton, New York 13809
(607) 764-8118

Rapid River Rustic Cedar
Log Homes & Fencing
Route 3, Ensign
Rapid River, Michigan 49878
(906) 474-6427

Raystown Land Company
R.D. No. 1, Box 29, Department "L"
James Creek, Pennsulvania 16657
(814) 658-3469

Rocky Mountain Log Homes
Montana Sundown, Inc.
3353 Highway 93 South
Hamilton, Montana 59840
(406) 363-5680

Rocky River Log Homes, Inc.
P.O. Box 992, 1411 Concord Avenue
Monroe, North Carolina 28110
(704) 283-2166/289-8517

Rustic Log Homes, Inc.
1207 Grover Road
P.O. Box 1133
Kings Mountain, North Carolina 28086
(704) 739-3613
800-222-9803

Satterwhite Log Homes
Route 2, Box 256A
Longview, Texas 75605
(214) 663-1729

Shawnee Log Homes, Inc.
Route 1, Box 123
Elliston, Virginia 24087
(703) 989-5400 or (703) 268-2244

Smokey Mountain Log Cabins, Inc.
P.O. Box 549
Maggie Valley, North Carolina 28751
(704) 926-0886

Smoky Gap Log Homes, Inc.
P.O. Box 562
Dallas, North Carolina 28034
800-222-LOGS (N.C.)
800-438-LOGS (U.S.)

Solid Wall Buildings, Inc.
P.O. Box 41
Newport, New Hampshire 03773
(603) 863-3107/3152

Southern Cypress Log Homes, Inc.
P.O. Box 209, U.S. Highway 19 S.
Crystal River, Florida 32629
(904) 795-0777

Southern Log Homes
  By Westerfield Ltd.
P.O. Box 236
Andrews, North Carolina 28901
(704) 321-4171

Southland Log Homes, Inc.
Rt. 2, Box 5B
Irmo, South Carolina 29063
(803) 781-5100

Sylvan Products, Inc.
4729 State Highway No. 3, S.W.
Port Orchard, Washington 98366
(206) 674-2511

Tennessee Log Buildings Inc.
Box 865
Athens, Tennessee 37303
(615) 745-8993
1-800-251-9218

Timber Log Homes, Inc.
21 LG Austin Drive, Box 300 LG
Marlborough, Connecticut 06447
(203) 295-9529

The Timber Touch
530C Searls Ave.
Nevada City, California 95959
(916) 273-7677

Town & Country Log Homes
4772 U.S. 131 South
Petoskey, Michigan 49770
(616) 347-4360

Traditional Living, Inc.
Real Log Homes
National Information Center
P.O. Box 202
Hartland, Vermont 05048
(800) 451-4485

Treehouse Log Homes, Inc.
801 South Garl, P.O. Box S 25
Burlington, Washington 98233
(206) 757-6066

Tri-Log Incorporated
Route 1, Box 4212
Twin Falls, Idaho 83301
(208) 734-1878

True Craft Log Structures Ltd.
7325 Mandeville St.
Burnaby, British Columbia V5J 4Z3
(604) 430-5351

Tukki Log Homes
A.J.L. Holdings Ltd.
P.O. Box 2790
The Pas, Manitoba R9A 1R1
(204) 624-5621

Tussey Mountain Log Homes, Inc.
2 Hirtzel Road
Warren, Pennsylvania 16365
(814) 723-9597 or (814) 563-7111

Uni-Log Precut Buildings
Div. of Calgary Sash & Door Ltd.
735-41st Ave., N.E.
Calgary, Alberta T2E 3P9
(403) 277-0771

Ward Cabin Company
P.O. Box 72
Houlton, Maine 04730
(207) 532-6531
1-800-341-1566

Western Log Homes
5201 W. 48th Avenue
Denver, Colorado 80212
(303) 455-0993

Wilderness Building Systems, Inc.
53 East Oakland Avenue
Salt Lake City, Utah 84114
(801) 466-6284, 485-1493

Wilderness Log Homes, Inc.
Route 2
Plymouth, Wisconsin 53073
(414) 893-8416

Wildewood Custom Log Homes, Inc.
Condon, Montana 59826
(406) 754-2222

Wisconsin Log Homes Inc.
P.O. Box 3793
Green Bay, Wisconsin 54303
(414) 865-7081

Yellowstone Log Homes
Route 4, Box 2
Rigby, Idaho 83442
(208) 745-8110/7193

Yesteryear Log Homes, Inc.
P.O. Box 1046
Mooresville, North Carolina 28115
(704) 932-0137

Youngstrom Log Homes
P.O. Box 356
Blackfoot, Idaho 83221
(208) 785-0632

Hand-Hewn Log Homes

Adaptive Restoration Company
Route 2, Connelly Road
Whitewater, Wisconsin 53190
(414) 495-4125

Adirondack Log Building—Design
and Consulting
(Krissa Johnson)
P.O. Box 300
Lake Clear, New York 12945
(518) 891-4507

Alaska Spruce Pole Craft
P.O. Box 58
Nenana, Alaska 99760

Alpine Log Homes, Inc.
P.O. Box 85
Victor, Montana 59875
(406) 642-3451

Appalachian Log Homes, Inc.
Hwy. 66, 1830 Winfield Dunn Pkwy.
Sevierville, Tennessee 37862
(615) 428-1325

Appalachian Log Structures
Appalachian Division
Burke-Parsons-Bowlby Corporation
Dept. LHG, P.O. Box 86
Goshen, Virginia 24439
(703) 997-9251

Ark II (John D. Keeling & Sons)
Box 149
Okanogan, Washington 98840
(509) 826-2310

Beaver Log Builders Ltd.
R.R. 4, Box 29
Johnstone Site
Quesnel, British Columbia V2J 3H8
(604) 992-5003

Blue Trail Log Homes
Blue Trail Construction Ltd.
Box 994,
Rocky Mountain House, Alberta T0M 1T0
(403) 845-4777/2530

Building with Logs Limited
Midhurst, Ontario L0L 1X0
(705) 726-1966

Handcrafted Log and Timber
Structures By
Timothy J. Bullock Co. Ltd.
RR 3, Creemore, Ontario L0M 1G0
(705) 466-2505

Ed Campbell Log Buildings
General Delivery
Celista, British Columbia V0E 1L0
(604) 955-2239

Custom Log Homes, Inc.
Drawer 226
Stevensville, Montana 59870
(406) 777-5202

John DeVries Log Homes
R.R. 3
Tweed, Ontario K0K 3J0
(613) 478-6830

Glenn Diezel Log & Timber Construction
Box 752
Minden Ontario K0M 2K0
(705) 754-2425

Jack Fast & Son Log Homes Ltd.
Box 400
Enderby, British Columbia V0E 1V0
(604) 838-6262

Tom Flegal
Pine Log Homes & Cottages
R.R. 2
Eganville, Ontario K0J 1M0
(613) 628-2372

Frontier Homes
1143 N.E. Willow Creek Road
Corvallis, Montana 59828
(406) 961-3115

Peter Gott Log Buildings
Route 3, Box 275
Marshall, North Carolina 28753
(704) 656-2521

Grown in Oregon Log Homes
P.O. Box 7316
Bend, Oregon 97708
(503) 388-4312

Handcrafted Log Homes By
Faulkner Log Construction
(Peter Faulkner)
R.R. 1
Goulais River, Ontario P0S 1E0
(705) 649-2312

Handcrafted Log Homes, Inc.
Route 1, Box 84-A
Atlantic Mine, Michigan 49905
(906) 482-8556

Hearthstone Builders, Inc.
Route 2, Box 434Z
Dandridge, Tennessee 37725
(615) 397-9425
also:
Route 2 Hwy 70
Kingston Springs, Tennessee 37082
(615) 244-6181

Highland Log Builders
P.O. Box 2686
Creston, B.C. V0B 1G0
(604) 428-9678

High Prairie Log Builders Ltd.
P.O. Box 1031
Oakridge, Oregon 97463
(503) 782-3117

Hutley Log Homes
R.R. 1
Huntsville, Ontario P0A 1K0
(705) 789-8443

Vic Janzen
Lindell Beach
c/o Chilliwack, British Columbia V0P 1P0
(604) 858-4135

Log Structures & Designs
  By Douglas Lukian
C.P. 1006
St. Sauveur, Quebec J0R 1R0
(514) 226-5952

Maple Island Log Homes
P.O. Box 331
Traverse City, Michigan 49685
(616) 821-2655/(616) 947-2164

Charles McRaven Restorations
Drawer G
Free Union, Virginia 22940
(804) 973-4859

Mountain Logs
P.O. Box 1128
Hamilton, Montana 59840
(406) 961-3222

Mountain Timber Log Homes, Inc.
Route 1, Box 5A
Hartford, Tennessee 37753
(615) 487-2242
1-800-345-LOGS (U.S.)
1-800-624-7214 (TN)

Northwest Log Homes Ltd.
P.O. Box 4714
Quesnel, British Columbia V2J 3J9
(604) 992-2442

The Original Log Homes
Box 1301
100 Mile House, British Columbia V0K 2E0
(604) 395-3868

Pacific Log Homes Ltd.
P.O. Box 80868
Burnaby, British Columbia V5H 3Y1
(604) 524-1577

Larry Parker Log Construction Limited
R.R. #1
Campbellcroft, Ontario L0A 1B0
(416) 797-2531

Gary Pendergrass—A Place In The Sun
Elsie Route 561
Seaside, Oregon 97138
(503) 755-2349

Paul Petric Construction Ltd.
Box 733
Minden, Ontario K0M 2K0
(705) 489-2233

Pinelodge Construction
P.O. Box 745
Parowan, Utah 84761
(801) 477-8137

Steve Pinther
Box 245
Ashton, Idaho 83420
(208) 652-3608

Pioneer Log Company
P.O. Box 1703
Auburn, California 95603
(916) 367-2731

Pioneer Logs Ltd.
R.R. 2,
Singhampton Ontario M0C 1M0
(519) 922-2836 or (705) 445-0923

Rustics of Lindbergh Lake, Inc.
Condon, Montana 59826
(406) 754-2222

Sawatzky Log Homes
Star Route Box 218
Cook, Minnesota 55723
(218) 666-5537

Southern Cypress Log Homes, Inc.
P.O. Box 209
Crystal River, Florida 32629
(904) 795-0777

Stonemill Log Homes, Inc.
7015 Stonemill Road
Knoxville, Tennessee 37919
(615) 693-4833

Superior Log Homes Inc.
5253 Corey Road
Williamstown, Michigan 48895
(517) 468-3344

Traditional Craftsmen
6464 Burleson Road
Oneida, New York 13421
(315) 363-2028

Webster Log Construction
Box 307, 150 Mile House
(Williams Lake), British Columbia V0K 2G0
(604) 296-3579

Wilderness Builders
P.O. Box 631
Bigfork, Montana 59911
(406) 837-LOGS (837-5647)

Pat Wolfe Log Homes
R.R. 1
McDonalds Corners, Ontario K0G 1M0
(613) 278-2009

W.P.M. Hand Crafted Log Homes
161 Ridgewood Terrace
St. Albert, Alberta T8N 0E9
(403) 458-4855

RECOMMENDED READING

Be Your Own House Contractor, Carl Heldman, Garden Way Publishing, Pownel, Vt., 1981.

Build Your Own Low-cost Log Home, Roger Hard, Garden Way Publishing, Pownel, Vt., 1977.

Carpentry: Some Tricks of the Trade from an Old-Style Carpenter, Bob Syvanen, The East Woods Press, Charlotte, NC, 1982.

The Energy Economics and Thermal Performance of Log Houses, Doris Muir & Paul Osborne, Muir Publishing Co., Ltd. (consumer edition, $5.00, technical edition, $15.00).

Interior Finish: More Tricks of the Trade from an Old-Style Carpenter, Bob Syvanen, The East Woods Press, Charlotte, N.C., 1982.

Log Home Design, Muir Publishing Co., Ltd. (special issue from *Log Home Guide*, $3.00).

Log Home Guide for Builders and Buyers, Muir Publishing Co. Ltd., 1 Pacific, Gardenvile, Que., Canada H9X 1B0. (514-457-2045) Published Spring, Summer, Fall, and Winter. (Annual Directory). (All four for $18.00; Winter Annual Directory, $10.00).

Manage Your Own Renovation Project, Carl Heldmann, Putnam, New York, 1983.

Your Log House, Vic Janzen, Muir Publishing Co., Ltd. ($15.00).

Glossary

BACKFILLING—Filling an area with dirt, sand or stone to bring it up to desired grade (level).

BATTER BOARDS—Boards erected to show the proper height and corners of a foundation.

BIDS—The amount of money for which a subcontractor is willing to do a specific job. Also, quotes.

BUILDING CODES—Sets of laws that establish minimum standards in construction. Codes and enforcement of compliance vary with locale.

CAPPING—Covering the ridge of a roof with roofing material.

CERTIFICATE OF INSURANCE—Proof of insurance.

CHECKING—Surface cracks in wood.

CHINKING—Closing up the gaps between the logs in a chink style log home.

CIRCUIT BREAKERS—Electrical devices that prevent overloading of an electrical circuit.

CLEAR TITLE—Proof of ownership of any property that is free of any encumbrances such as liens, mortgages, judgments, etc.

COLLATERAL—Physical property pledged as repayment of a loan.

CONTRACTS—Agreed upon quotes or bids by you and the subcontractor and put in writing.

DEED—A legal document that transfers ownership of property.

DORMER—A window or even a room, projecting from a sloping roof.

DRAWS—Disbursements of money that equal a percentage of the total amount due.

DRYING-IN—Term indicating that your house is far enough along as to be protected from rain or snow. Also called "in the dry" and "weather tight."

EXPANSION JOINT—A joint in concrete to allow for expansion of the concrete with temperature changes. It is usually made of fiber board or styrofoam.

FACIA—Also, facia board. The trim board around a roof's edge.

FLASHING—Sheets of metal used to weatherproof roof joints.

FOOTINGS—The basis of a structure, usually made of concrete, that supports the foundation of a house.

FRAMING MEMBERS—The materials used to put the house together—other than the logs.

GABLE—The triangular wall formed by the sloping ends of a ridged roof.

HEAT GAIN—A term used to describe heat entering a building.

HEAT LOSS—A term used to describe heat escaping from a building.

LETTER OF COMMITMENT—A letter from a permanent lender stating that they will make a permanent loan to you, provided that all the conditions that led them to this decision are the same at the time of closing. Its purpose is to allow you to obtain construction financing.

LIEN WAIVER—A legal document that states than an individual or firm has been paid in full for the labor or supplies that went into your home.

LOAD BEARING—Capable of carrying the weight of a structure.

LOT SUBORDINATION—A process of buying land whereby the entire purchase price does not have to be paid in order to receive a deed to the land. The seller takes a promissory note or a (second) mortgage and subordinates his rights to those of the construction loan lender.

MANAGER'S CONTRACT—A contract with a professional general contractor whereby he will manage as much of and as many of the phases of construction as you wish, with you remaining as the overall general contractor.

PLOT PLAN—A survey of your land showing where the house will be positioned.

POINTS—A charge for lending money.

QUALIFY—A term that means one can afford a mortgage.

QUOTES—See Bids.

RECORDED—On file at the local county courthouse, usually attached to a deed.

RECORDING FEES—The fees charged to record a legal document.

RESTRICTIONS—Certain restraints placed on a particular lot or parcel of land, by the current owner or a previous owner. Size of house, architectural design, number of stories, type of driveway, use of out-buildings, etc., are some of the things covered by restrictions.

RIDGE VENT—A continuous vent that runs along the ridge (peak) of a roof.

ROUGH-IN—The installation of wiring, plumbing, heat ducts, etc., in the walls, floors or ceilings (before those walls, floors or ceilings) are covered up permanently.

SASH LOCKS—Window locks.

SAW BOX—Temporary electrical service receptacle.

SAW SERVICE—Temporary electrical service for the purpose of construction.

SILL PLATE—The horizontal framing member, next to the foundation that supports a wall or floor.

SOFFIT—The underside of a roof's overhang, or cornice.

SUB FLOOR—The floor beneath the finished or final floor. Usually ½" plywood.

SURVEY—A written description of a lot or parcel of land that determines its location and boundaries.

TAKE-OFF—An estimate of materials.

THERMAL MASS—The bulk of logs, stone or masonry that inhibits the passage of heat through the walls.

TITLE—Proof of ownership.

WINDOW GRIDS—The mullions or dividers that snap into place to look like window panes. Used with insulated glass windows that don't have panes.

WOOD FOUNDATION—A foundation made of treated wood in lieu of masonry or concrete. Can be installed even in frigid weather.

ZONING—An area of land that is restricted by a local government to a certain use, such as residential, business, industrial, etc.

East Woods Press Books

Backcountry Cooking
Berkshire Trails for Walking & Ski Touring
Best Bed & Breakfast in the World, The
California Bed & Breakfast
Campfire Chillers
Campfire Songs
Canoeing the Jersey Pine Barrens
Carolina Curiosities
Carolina Seashells
Carpentry: Some Tricks of the Trade from an Old-Style Carpenter
Catfish Cookbook, The
Charlotte: A Touch of Gold
Complete Guide to Backpacking in Canada
Creative Gift Wrapping
Day Trips From Cincinnati
Day Trips From Houston
Drafting: Tips and Tricks on Drawing and Designing House Plans
Exploring Nova Scotia
Fifty Years on the Fifty: The Orange Bowl Story
Fructose Cookbook, The
Grand Strand: An Uncommon Guide to Myrtle Beach, The
Healthy Trail Food Book, The
Hiking from Inn to Inn
Hiking Virginia's National Forests
Historic Country House Hotels
Hosteling USA, Third Edition
How to Play With Your Baby
Interior Finish: More Tricks of the Trade
Just Folks: Visitin' with Carolina People
Kays Gary, Columnist
Maine Coast: A Nature Lover's Guide, The
Making Food Beautiful
Mid-Atlantic Guest House Book, The
New England Guest House Book, The
New England: Off the Beaten Path
Ohio: Off the Beaten Path
Parent Power!
Race, Rock and Religion
Rocky Mountain National Park Hiking Trails
Saturday Notebook, The
Sea Islands of the South
South Carolina Hiking Trails
Southern Guest House Book, The
Southern Rock: A Climber's Guide to the South
Sweets Without Guilt
Tar Heel Sights: Guide to North Carolina's Heritage
Tennessee Trails
Train Trips: Exploring America by Rail
Trout Fishing the Southern Appalachians
Vacationer's Guide to Orlando and Central Florida, A
Walks in the Catskills
Walks in the Great Smokies
Walks with Nature in Rocky Mountain National Park
Whitewater Rafting in Eastern America
Woman's Journey, A
You Can't Live on Radishes

Order from:

The East Woods Press
429 East Boulevard
Charlotte, NC 28203

Notes

Notes

Notes